TExES School Librarian
150 Teacher Certification Exam

D1252240

By: Sharon Wynne, M.S.
Southern Connecticut State University

"And, while there's no reason yet to panic, I think it's only prudent that we make preparations to panic."

XAMonline, INC.
Boston

Copyright © 2007 XAMonline, Inc.
All rights reserved. No part of the material protected by this copyright notice may be reproduced or utilized in any form or by any means, electronic or mechanical, including photocopying, recording or by any information storage and retrievable system, without written permission from the copyright holder.

To obtain permission(s) to use the material from this work for any purpose including workshops or seminars, please submit a written request to:

XAMonline, Inc.
21 Orient Ave.
Melrose, MA 02176
Toll Free 1-800-509-4128
Email: info@xamonline.com
Web www.xamonline.com
Fax: 1-781-662-9268

Library of Congress Cataloging-in-Publication Data

Wynne, Sharon A.
    School Librarian 150: Teacher Certification / Sharon A. Wynne. -2nd ed.
    ISBN 978-1-58197-940-4
        1. School Librarian 150.   2. Study Guides.   3. TExES
        4. Teachers' Certification & Licensure.   5. Careers

Disclaimer:
The opinions expressed in this publication are the sole works of XAMonline and were created independently from the National Education Association, Educational Testing Service, or any State Department of Education, National Evaluation Systems or other testing affiliates.

Between the time of publication and printing, state specific standards as well as testing formats and website information may change that is not included in part or in whole within this product. Sample test questions are developed by XAMonline and reflect similar content as on real tests; however, they are not former tests. XAMonline assembles content that aligns with state standards but makes no claims nor guarantees teacher candidates a passing score. Numerical scores are determined by testing companies such as NES or ETS and then are compared with individual state standards. A passing score varies from state to state.

Printed in the United States of America   œ-1

TExES: School Librarian 150
ISBN: 978-1-58197-940-4

Table of Contents

pg.

DOMAIN I. **TEACHING, LEARNING, AND THE SCHOOL LIBRARY ENVIRONMENT**

COMPETENCY 001 **(TEACHING AND LEARNING IN THE SCHOOL LIBRARY PROGRAM) THE SCHOOL LIBRARIAN UNDERSTANDS TEACHING AND LEARNING PROCESSES AND PROMOTES THE INTEGRATION OF CURRICULUM, RESOURCES, AND TEACHING STRATEGIES TO ENSURE ALL STUDENTS' SUCCESS AS CREATORS AND USERS OF IDEAS AND INFORMATION** 1

Skill 1.1   Participates as an educational leader, an equal partner, and a change agent in the curriculum development process at both the campus and district levels 1

Skill 1.2   Understands curriculum design and participates in integrated planning of a shared campus vision that focuses on reading, teaching, and learning 2

Skill 1.3   Uses collaborative planning, cooperative teaching, and direct instruction, as determined by students' needs and state curriculum standards..3

Skill 1.4   Teaches students effective strategies to locate, gather, select, synthesize, and evaluate information 4

Skill 1.5   Instructs students in the ethical use of information resources (e.g., plagiarism, copyright, acceptable use) 5

Skill 1.6   Collaborates with faculty to design instructional activities that foster independent learning...7

Skill 1.7   Adapts teaching strategies to address the diverse learning needs and varied cultural backgrounds of the student population.............7

Skill 1.8   Provides and promotes ongoing staff development/continuing professional education (e.g., integration of information technology, information literacy, literature appreciation) for the learning community 8

Skill 1.9   Provides and promotes ongoing learning opportunities (e.g., integration of information technology, information literacy, literature appreciation) for students 9

Skill 1.10 Directs and encourages students to read, view, experience, and listen to a variety of fiction and nonfiction resources for personal and informational needs 10

COMPETENCY 002   (LIBRARY ENVIRONMENT) THE SCHOOL LIBRARIAN ESTABLISHES A LIBRARY ENVIRONMENT THAT ENABLES AND ENCOURAGES ALL MEMBERS OF THE LEARNING COMMUNITY TO EXPLORE AND MEET THEIR INFORMATION NEEDS 13

Skill 2.1   Understands principles of exemplary library design as defined by state and federal guidelines for a simultaneous-use facility for individuals, small groups, and classes 13

Skill 2.2   Develops and maintains a flexible, functional, and barrier-free library facility that is safe, secure, and age-appropriate 15

Skill 2.3   Uses space effectively in the school library (e.g., for displays of student-produced, faculty-produced, and community-produced materials and collections) 15

Skill 2.4   Promotes equitable access to resources and information during and beyond the instructional day and school year 15

Skill 2.5   Creates a learning environment in which the diversity of groups and the uniqueness of individuals are recognized and appreciated 16

Skill 2.6   Provides access to library resources and facilities through open, flexible scheduling for classes, small groups, and individuals 17

DOMAIN II.   PROGRAM MANAGEMENT, LEADERSHIP, AND CONNECTIONS TO THE COMMUNITY

COMPETENCY 003   (LIBRARY PROGRAM MANAGEMENT) THE SCHOOL LIBRARIAN UNDERSTANDS LIBRARY PROGRAM MANAGEMENT AND ACQUIRES, ORGANIZES, AND MANAGES RESOURCES 18

Skill 3.1   Uses effective decision making (e.g., synthesizing information from a variety of sources) to develop and maintain an exemplary library program 18

Skill 3.2   Develops procedures for the school library program to ensure compliance with Board policies and local, state, and federal laws 19

Skill 3.3   Uses effective strategies and techniques for systematically performing fiscal library management operations (e.g., record keeping, budgeting, purchasing, grant writing) 21

Skill 3.4   Manages and maintains facilities and resources (e.g., scheduling, circulation, inventory, repair, reporting) 23

Skill 3.5   Supervises students and implements programs to manage and evaluate human resources 25

Skill 3.6   Collaborates with faculty to evaluate (e.g., select, weed) library resources that support the curriculum and leisure reading 28

Skill 3.7   Designs and implements acceptable use policies for current and emerging technologies 29

Skill 3.8   Monitors, assesses, and employs existing and emerging technologies for management applications 30

Skill 3.9   Uses effective planning, time management, and organization of work to maximize attainment of district and campus goals 31

COMPETENCY 004   (LIBRARY PROGRAM LEADERSHIP AND
                   CONNECTIONS . TO THE COMMUNITY) THE SCHOOL
                   LIBRARIAN EXHIBITS LIBRARY PROGRAM
                   LEADERSHIP AND COLLABORATES WITHIN THE
                   SCHOOL AND COMMUNITY TO PROMOTE THE
                   SUCCESS OF ALL STUDENTS 38

Skill 4.1   Advocates for the development of an exemplary library program
              that encourages excellence in all students 38

Skill 4.2   Designs and uses statistical reports to support an exemplary library
              program 38

Skill 4.3   Applies effective leadership strategies within campus and district
              administrative structures to promote library program goals 39

Skill 4.4   Promotes awareness of, respect for, and responsiveness to
              learning differences and diversity within the school and community
              40

Skill 4.5   Communicates effectively through oral, written, electronic, and
              nonverbal expression 40

Skill 4.6   Establishes partnerships with businesses, learning institutions,
              global communities, organizations, and other libraries to strengthen
              programs and support campus goals 40

Skill 4.7   Develops library programs that offer families opportunities to
              participate in school activities and in their children's education
              41

Skill 4.8   Develops and implements a comprehensive public relations
              program (e.g., news media, Web pages, newsletters) that
              effectively involves and informs multiple constituencies 42

DOMAIN III.   **LIBRARIANSHIP, INFORMATION SCIENCE, AND TECHNOLOGY**

COMPETENCY 005   **(LIBRARIANSHIP AND INFORMATION SCIENCE) THE SCHOOL LIBRARIAN APPLIES KNOWLEDGE OF LIBRARIANSHIP AND INFORMATION SCIENCE TO HELP THE SCHOOL COMMUNITY LOCATE, EVALUATE, AND USE INFORMATION TO SOLVE PROBLEMS AND TO ENCOURAGE LIFELONG READING AND LEARNING 43**

Skill 5.1   Understands the role of all types of libraries and information agencies in an integrated learning environment 43

Skill 5.2   Understands the role of the school library program as a central element in the intellectual life of the school 44

Skill 5.3   Applies knowledge of theories, principles, and skills related to collection development (e.g., evaluating, selecting, and acquiring resources) 45

Skill 5.4   Applies standard procedures (e.g., AACR, Dewey, LCSH, MARC) for classifying, cataloging, and processing resources 51

Skill 5.5   Applies knowledge of theories, principles, and skills related to organization, storage, and retrieval of resources 51

Skill 5.6   Applies bibliographic and retrieval techniques for organizing and using information sources 52

Skill 5.7   Effectively interviews patrons to determine information needs 53

Skill 5.8   Applies knowledge of literature and information resources to help patrons select materials 54

Skill 5.9   Employs a variety of techniques (e.g., reading materials, media, programs, motivational strategies) to guide the development of independent readers 56

Skill 5.10   Understands and applies principles of ethical behavior (e.g., intellectual freedom, information access, privacy, intellectual property) in various professional contexts 56

Skill 5.11   Demonstrates a commitment to the library profession (e.g., membership in professional organizations, participation in continuing education, collaboration with other information professionals) 58

COMPETENCY 006   (INFORMATION ACCESS AND TECHNOLOGY) THE SCHOOL LIBRARIAN USES AND INTEGRATES TECHNOLOGY, TELECOMMUNICATIONS, AND INFORMATION SYSTEMS TO ENRICH THE CURRICULUM, ENHANCE LEARNING, AND PROMOTE THE SUCCESS OF THE SCHOOL COMMUNITY 59

Skill 6.1   Understands basic terms and concepts of current technology (e.g., hardware, software applications and functions, input/output devices, networks)...59

Skill 6.2   Evaluates, acquires, analyzes, and manages digital resources (e.g., databases, network information) and assesses information for accuracy and validity 60

Skill 6.3   Uses existing and emerging technologies to access, evaluate, and disseminate information for library and instructional programs......60

Skill 6.4   Uses interlibrary loan to facilitate information access beyond the campus..62

Skill 6.5   Uses productivity tools to communicate information in various formats (e.g., newsletters, multimedia presentations, Web applications, teleconferencing) 62

Skill 6.6   Uses information problem-solving processes, activities, and materials to integrate the state-mandated curriculum for technology applications into the library program...63

Skill 6.7   Models successful search strategies using technology 63

Skill 6.8   Guides students and staff to utilize established criteria (e.g., design, content delivery, audience, relevance) in the development of technology-based products 64

Skill 6.9   Participates in district, state, and national technology initiatives 67

Skill 6.10   Selects and utilizes automation systems, including OPAC on the Web, to provide maximum access to resources. 67

Sample Test..**68**

Answer Key **100**

Rigor Table **101**

Rationales with Sample Questions **102**

Great Study and Testing Tips!

What to study in order to prepare for the subject assessments is the focus of this study guide but equally important is *how* you study.

You can increase your chances of truly mastering the information by taking some simple, but effective steps.

Study Tips:

1. **Some foods aid the learning process.** Foods such as milk, nuts, seeds, rice, and oats help your study efforts by releasing natural memory enhancers called CCKs (*cholecystokinin*) composed of *tryptophan*, *choline*, and *phenylalanine*. All of these chemicals enhance the neurotransmitters associated with memory. Before studying, try a light, protein-rich meal of eggs, turkey, and fish. All of these foods release the memory enhancing chemicals. The better the connections, the more you comprehend.

Likewise, before you take a test, stick to a light snack of energy boosting and relaxing foods. A glass of milk, a piece of fruit, or some peanuts all release various memory-boosting chemicals and help you to relax and focus on the subject at hand.

2. **Learn to take great notes.** A by-product of our modern culture is that we have grown accustomed to getting our information in short doses (i.e. TV news sound bites or USA Today style newspaper articles.)

Consequently, we've subconsciously trained ourselves to assimilate information better in neat little packages. If your notes are scrawled all over the paper, it fragments the flow of the information. Strive for clarity. Newspapers use a standard format to achieve clarity. Your notes can be much clearer through use of proper formatting. A very effective format is called the *"Cornell Method."*

> Take a sheet of loose-leaf lined notebook paper and draw a line all the way down the paper about 1-2" from the left-hand edge.

> Draw another line across the width of the paper about 1-2" up from the bottom. Repeat this process on the reverse side of the page.

Look at the highly effective result. You have ample room for notes, a left hand margin for special emphasis items or inserting supplementary data from the textbook, a large area at the bottom for a brief summary, and a little rectangular space for just about anything you want.

3. <u>Get the concept then the details</u>. Too often we focus on the details and don't gather an understanding of the concept. However, if you simply memorize only dates, places, or names, you may well miss the whole point of the subject.

A key way to understand things is to put them in your own words. If you are working from a textbook, automatically summarize each paragraph in your mind. If you are outlining text, don't simply copy the author's words.

Rephrase them in your own words. You remember your own thoughts and words much better than someone else's, and subconsciously tend to associate the important details to the core concepts.

4. <u>Ask Why?</u> Pull apart written material paragraph by paragraph and don't forget the captions under the illustrations.

Example: If the heading is "Stream Erosion", flip it around to read "Why do streams erode?" Then answer the questions.

If you train your mind to think in a series of questions and answers, not only will you learn more, but it also helps to lessen the test anxiety because you are used to answering questions.

5. <u>Read for reinforcement and future needs</u>. Even if you only have 10 minutes, put your notes or a book in your hand. Your mind is similar to a computer; you have to input data in order to have it processed. *By reading, you are creating the neural connections for future retrieval.* The more times you read something, the more you reinforce the learning of ideas.

Even if you don't fully understand something on the first pass, *your mind stores much of the material for later recall.*

6. <u>Relax to learn so go into exile</u>. Our bodies respond to an inner clock called biorhythms. Burning the midnight oil works well for some people, but not everyone.

If possible, set aside a particular place to study that is free of distractions. Shut off the television, cell phone, and pager and exile your friends and family during your study period.

If you really are bothered by silence, try background music. Light classical music at a low volume has been shown to aid in concentration over other types. Music that evokes pleasant emotions without lyrics is highly suggested. Try just about anything by Mozart. It relaxes you.

7. **Use arrows not highlighters.** At best, it's difficult to read a page full of yellow, pink, blue, and green streaks. Try staring at a neon sign for a while and you'll soon see that the horde of colors obscure the message.

A quick note, a brief dash of color, an underline, and an arrow pointing to a particular passage is much clearer than a horde of highlighted words.

8. **Budget your study time.** Although you shouldn't ignore any of the material, *allocate your available study time in the same ratio that topics may appear on the test.*

Testing Tips:

1. Get smart, play dumb. Don't read anything into the question. Don't make an assumption that the test writer is looking for something else than what is asked. Stick to the question as written and don't read extra things into it.

2. Read the question and all the choices *twice* before answering the question. You may miss something by not carefully reading, and then re-reading both the question and the answers.

If you really don't have a clue as to the right answer, leave it blank on the first time through. Go on to the other questions, as they may provide a clue as to how to answer the skipped questions.

If later on, you still can't answer the skipped ones . . . *Guess.* The only penalty for guessing is that you *might* get it wrong. Only one thing is certain; if you don't put anything down, you will get it wrong!

3. Turn the question into a statement. Look at the way the questions are worded. The syntax of the question usually provides a clue. Does it seem more familiar as a statement rather than as a question? Does it sound strange?

By turning a question into a statement, you may be able to spot if an answer sounds right, and it may also trigger memories of material you have read.

4. Look for hidden clues. It's actually very difficult to compose multiple-foil (choice) questions without giving away part of the answer in the options presented.

In most multiple-choice questions you can often readily eliminate one or two of the potential answers. This leaves you with only two real possibilities and automatically your odds go to Fifty-Fifty for very little work.

5. Trust your instincts. For every fact that you have read, you subconsciously retain something of that knowledge. On questions that you aren't really certain about, go with your basic instincts. **Your first impression on how to answer a question is usually correct.**

6. Mark your answers directly on the test booklet. Don't bother trying to fill in the optical scan sheet on the first pass through the test.

Just be very careful not to miss-mark your answers when you eventually transcribe them to the scan sheet.

7. Watch the clock! You have a set amount of time to answer the questions. Don't get bogged down trying to answer a single question at the expense of 10 questions you can more readily answer.

THIS PAGE BLANK

DOMAIN I.   **TEACHING, LEARNING, AND**
                                       THE SCHOOL LIBRARY ENVIRONMENT

COMPETENCY 1   **(TEACHING AND LEARNING IN THE SCHOOL LIBRARY PROGRAM) THE SCHOOL LIBRARIAN UNDERSTANDS TEACHING AND LEARNING PROCESSES AND PROMOTES THE INTEGRATION OF CURRICULUM, RESOURCES, AND TEACHING STRATEGIES TO ENSURE ALL STUDENTS' SUCCESS AS CREATORS AND USERS OF IDEAS AND INFORMATION.**

Skill 1.1   **Participates as an educational leader, an equal partner, and a change agent in the curriculum development process at both the campus and district levels.**

The school library media specialist plays a vital leadership role within the school community. They pose a strong influence in curriculum and instructional areas as they provide an informational link to all areas through their thorough knowledge of TEKS and all state curricula.

They serve as a link to educational reform. School library media specialists touch all parts of the learning community. They work closely with administrators, teachers, parents and other community members to design a media program that furthers the school's mission and goals.

Much of the leadership exerted by a school library media specialist comes from serving as a resource and coaching others to learn and do for themselves. They provide staff development in various formats as well as provide opportunities for parents to support their child's education.

The school library media specialist proactively seeks ways to promote the media program by seeking partnerships within the community. Through partnerships they increase the resources available to the students as well as gain support for the program itself.

A good leader should be able to work and inspire others to work in a team environment where the input of team members at all levels is encouraged and appreciated. To accomplish this goal, she should:

1.   Exhibit the desire to achieve the goals of an efficient library media program.
2.   Show appreciation for the contributions of library media staff and supervise them in a democratic style.
3.   Delegate tasks to responsible staff members.
4.   Engage in continuing education.
5.   Maintain active membership in professional organizations.
6.   Show respect and concern for colleagues and superiors.

As with any good leader they share an equal load in attaining the overall mission and goals of the school. The school library media specialist works collaboratively with teachers to integrate information skills into core curriculum areas. They often model lessons for teachers and team teach activities. It is important that they work closely with teachers to administer the Texas Primary Reading Inventory (TPRI) and analyze results to improve reading.

Though the leadership of the school library media specialist may not be as visible as that of a school principal, they still play a key role in the school community.

Skill 1.2 **Understands curriculum design and participates in integrated planning of a shared campus vision that focuses on reading, teaching, and learning.**

School library media specialist plays a vital role in curriculum design and directing the vision of a school. *School Library Programs: Standards and Guidelines for Texas* strongly emphasize the importance of collaboration between the library media specialist and the classroom teacher.

As a team member, the school library media specialist contributes by

1.   Advising of current trends and studies in curriculum design.
2.   Advising the school staff on the use of media and instructional techniques to meet learning objectives.
3.   Ensuring that a systematic approach to information skills instruction will be included in curriculum plans.
4.   Recommending media and technologies appropriate to particular subject matter and activities.

Instructional planning for the school library media specialist is the process of effectively integrating library skills instruction into the curriculum.

Methods of instructional planning:

1.   Identify content. Teachers create a list of instructional objectives for specific classes. Library media specialists, using state and local scope and sequence, prepare a list of objectives for teaching information skills.
2.   Specify learning objectives. Teachers and library media specialists working together should merge the list of objectives
3.   Examine available resources.
4.   Determine instructional factors:
      a.   Learner styles.
      b.   Teaching techniques and teacher and library media specialist division of responsibilities in the lesson implementation.
      c.   Student groupings. Consider abilities, special needs, etc.
5.   Pretest.

6.   Determine activities to meet objectives.
7.   Select specific resources and support agencies.
8.   Implement the unit.
9.   Evaluate.
10.   Revise the objectives and/or activities.

Skill 1.3   Uses collaborative planning, cooperative teaching, and direct instruction, as determined by students' needs and state curriculum standards.

One of the single most important parts of a successful school library media program is collaboration between the school library media specialist and classroom teachers.

To support the collaborative process there are key skills the media specialist must possess. These include:

- Flexibility – have the ability to adjust to the differing needs of staff and students and flexibility with time
- Curriculum Expert – get to know the curriculum being taught at the grade levels being served. This makes the media specialist and invaluable partner.
- Leadership – set the path in which the media program should move towards, set goals and expectations, be the advocate for the teachers as well as the media program
- Approachable – establish good rapport with staff and students. Be someone they know will be willing to go above and beyond
- Persistence- to keep going and keep the media program moving forward

As a library media specialist works collaboratively with the classroom teacher their main focus is to create lessons and activities that integrate information skills into the curriculum.   Achievement of the design of collaborative teaching units with supplemental or total involvement of the library media center resources and services satisfy levels 9 and 10 of Loertscher's eleven level taxonomy   The taxonomy assumes the active involvement of the school library media specialist in the total school program.

Developing lifelong readers plays an important role in the library media program. The library media specialists works closely with the teacher to teach students how to locate and use information. They also work to develop a love for literature through literature enrichment activities like book talks and reading promotions. Individual learning styles based on theories such as Howard Gardner's Multiple Intelligences are taken into consideration and they work.

Skill 1.4   Teaches students effective strategies to locate, gather, select, synthesize, and evaluate information.

For students to be truly information literate they need to be armed with strategies that will guide them through the abundance of resources they are able to access. There are many information literacy models that help students to learn the process of locating and using resources effectively.

One of the most commonly used is the Big6 model. It was created by educators Mike Eisenberg and Bob Berkowitz. The Big6 process outlines how people solve an information problem. They have broken down this process into six stages.

1. Task Definition – identify problem and information needed

2. Information Seeking Strategies – decide on sources of information and select the best

3. Location and Access – locate the sources and search for the information

4. Use of Information – interact with the information and pick out that which is most relevant

5. Synthesis – organize the information and present it

6. Evaluation – evaluate its effectiveness of the product and the process

Another popular model is the Independent Investigation Method (IIM) from Active Learning. This seven step process involves:

1. Selecting a topic

2. Setting goals

3. Conducting research

4. Organizing information

5. Evaluating goals based upon the information found

6. Creating a product

7. Presenting the information

Skill 1.5   Instructs students in the ethical use of information resources (e.g., plagiarism, copyright, acceptable use).

The advent of technology that made copying print and non-print media efficient poses serious concern for educators who unwittingly or otherwise violate copyright law on a regular basis. Copyright laws stated very simply protect a work against unauthorized copying. Regardless of their intentions to provide their students access to materials that may be too costly for mass purchase, educators must understand the reasons for copyright protection and they must, by example, ensure the upholding of that protection.

Educators and students alike must be schooled in the basics of copyright laws. Though all educators should be cognizant of the law, it becomes the responsibility of the school library media specialist to help inform colleagues and monitor the proper application of the law.

Since some material is relevant to curricular topics, Fair Use Guidelines have been established to allow the use of copyright materials for educational purposes. Students and educators have the benefit of greater leeway in copying than any other group. Students and teachers should still take steps to guard against plagiarism, the stealing of another's ideas and presenting them as your own. Many print instructional materials do carry statements that allow production of multiple copies for classroom use, provided they adhere to the "Guidelines for Classroom Copying in Nonprofit Educational Institutions." Teachers may duplicate enough copies to provide one per student per course provided that they meet the tests of brevity, spontaneity, and cumulative effect.

1.   Brevity test:
      Poetry - suggested maximum 250 words.
      Prose - one complete essay, story, or article less than 2500 words <u>or</u> excerpts of no more than 1000 words or 10% of the work, whichever is less. (Children's books with text under 2500 words may not be copied in their entirety. No more than two pages containing 10% of the text may be copied.)
      Illustration - charts, drawings, cartoons, etc. are limited to one per book or periodical article.
2.   Spontaneity test: Normally copying that does not fall under the brevity test requires publisher's permission for duplication. However, allowances are made if "the inspiration and decision to use the work" occur too soon prior to classroom use for permission to be sought in writing.

3.   Cumulative effect test: Even in the case of short poems or prose, it is preferable to make only one copy. However, three short items from one work are allowable during one class term. Reuse of copied material from term to term is expressly forbidden. Compilation of works into anthologies to be used in place of purchasing texts is prohibited.

Copyright legislation has existed in the United States for more than 100 years. Conflicts over copyright were settled in the courts. The 1976 Copyright Act, especially section 107 dealing with Fair Use, created legislative criteria to follow based on judicial precedents. In 1978, when the law took effect, it set regulations for duration and scope of copyright, specified author rights, and set monetary penalties for infringement. The statutory penalty may be waived by the court for an employee of a non-profit educational institution where the employee can prove fair use intent.

Fair use is meant to create a balance between copyright protection and the needs of learners for access to protected material. Fair use is judged by the purpose of the use, the nature of the work (whether creative or informational), the quantity of the work for use, and the market effect.

In essence, if a <u>portion</u> of a work is used to benefit the learner with no intent to deprive the author of his profits, fair use is granted. Recently, Fair Use has been challenged most in cases of videotaping off-air of television programs. Guidelines, too numerous to delineate here affect copying audio-visual materials and computer software. Most distributors place written regulations in the packaging of these products. Allowances for single back-up copies in the event of damage to the original are granted.

Section 108 is pertinent to libraries in that it permits reproducing a single copy of an entire work if no financial gain is derived, if the library is public or archival, and if the copyright notice appears on all copies.

As stated earlier, technology has opened up a new avenue in which students can access resources. It is more important than ever to teach students ethical behavior for use in such circumstances. To address such concerns many districts have established Acceptable Use Policies.

An Acceptable Use Policy is a set of guidelines by which students and staff are to use network and web resources within the district. It outlines ethical behavior and the consequences for the misuse of the resources. Many locations have all those who wish to use their electronic services sign an agreement which states they will follow the guidelines and that they are aware of the consequences.

Skill 1.6   Collaborates with faculty to design instructional activities that foster independent learning.

To promote independent student learning the school library media specialist must work collaboratively with staff and students to teach information literacy skills. These tools are the stepping stones to self-directed and independent learning.

The school library media specialist plays an essential role by providing physical and intellectual access to resources. Through physical access patrons are able to locate a wide variety of resources quickly and easily. Special attention is paid to providing alternate formats to support student needs. By providing intellectual access to resources there is a wide array of topics to satisfy curiosity and to allow students to explore topics of interest.

Independence begins with a student questioning the world around them and being willing to seek answers. The school library media specialist can foster this through:

- Modeling the strategies that will teach students to be independent learners.
- Collaborate with teachers to develop effective strategies.
- Promoting the correct steps to take when working through an information literacy model.

Skill 1.7   Adapts teaching strategies to address the diverse learning needs and varied cultural backgrounds of the student population.

Each learning setting provides its own unique population with their own unique needs. It is important for the school library media specialist to work closely with teachers to ensure they provide a diverse collection of resources. The resources should address learning styles, a wide range of ability levels, physical needs, diversity of cultures and collections for various populations within the school such as students, teachers, and administrators.

To best address the needs of the student population it is important that the library media specialists assess their needs in relation to literacy and technology. There are several tools available to assess school needs. Basic tools such as surveys, observations, and interest inventories can be created and used. There are other more specific statewide tools in place to further assess needs:

- The Texas Primary Reading Inventory (TPRI) is used to measure a student's reading progress throughout the year. The school library media specialist can work closely with teachers to use this information to improve reading.
- The STaR Chart is designed to assess the technology needs of the school.

A deciding factor in meeting student needs is to have a flexibly scheduled media center. Having a flexible schedule allows students to receive help and guidance at the point of need. It also provides the library media specialist with time to collaboratively plan with teachers.

Skill 1.8   **Provides and promotes ongoing staff development/continuing professional education (e.g., integration of information technology, information literacy, literature appreciation) for the learning community.**

Staff, including teachers and support personnel, should be offered periodic in-service in learning new skills and reinforcing known skills. These skills may be taught at formal, structured workshops or in informal small-group or individual sessions when a need arises.

Sample activities include:

1.   A hands-on orientation for teachers new to school - to familiarize them with available resource and equipment and apprise them of services - should include information on incorporating appropriate media into their lessons. Written procedures for selection and evaluation should be available
2.   Provide information on new/existing media and solicit recommendations.
   a.   Send bibliographies, catalogs, or newsletters frequently, asking for purchase suggestions.
   b.   Inform all teachers of district and school preview policies and arrange previews for purchase suggestions.
   c.   Involve as many teachers as possible on review committees.
3.   Provide periodic brief refresher modules. Advertise the media and equipment to be used in each session. Suggest uses of each lesson's media format so teachers can make appropriate choices. Have teachers create one or more products at each session that can be used for instruction in an upcoming lesson.
4.   Secure oral or written feedback on both teacher-made and commercial media used in classroom lessons. Ask them to use appropriate evaluation criteria in measuring the product's worth. The more familiar they become with the criteria, the better their product choices will become.

Designing a staff development activity follows a basic lesson profile with special considerations for adult learners.

1.   Analyze learner styles. Adult learners are more receptive to role playing and individual performance before a group. Learner motivation is more internal, but some external motivations, such as release time, compensatory time, in service credit or some written recognition, might be discussed with the principal.
2.   Assess learner needs. Conduct a survey among teachers to determine which media or equipment they want to learn more about. Consider

environmental factors - time, place, temperature. Since many in service activities occur after school, taking the lesson to the teachers in their own classrooms may make them more comfortable especially if they can have a reviving afternoon snack. If they must come to the media center, serve refreshments.

3. Select performance objectives. Determine exactly what the teacher should be able to do at the end of a successful in service session.
4. Plan activities to achieve objectives. Demonstrate the skill to be taught, involve the participants in active performance/ production, and allow for practice and feedback.
5. Select appropriate resources. Arrange that all materials and equipment are ready and in good functioning order on the day of the in service.
6. Determine instructor. Either the school library media specialist or a faculty member should conduct these on-site in services unless the complexity or novelty of the technology requires an outside expert.
7. Provide continuing support. The instructor or designated substitute should be available after the in service for reinforcement.
8. Evaluation. Determine the effectiveness of the in service and make modifications as recommended in future in services

Because we are in the business of teaching, all technologies must be viewed as educational tools. To enable teachers to understand the way these technologies can be integrated into their teaching, they must understand the relationship between these tools and learning needs. The school library media professionals must be able to update teachers on this correlation.

1. Conduct timely, short inservice activities to demonstrate and allow teachers to manipulate new technologies and plan classroom uses.
2. Model the use of the technology used during integrated lessons.
2. Clip articles or write reviews to distribute to teachers with suggestions for application in their particular learning environment.
3. Offer to plan and teach lessons in different content areas.

Skill 1.9 Provides and promotes ongoing learning opportunities (e.g., integration of information technology, information literacy, literature appreciation) for students.

Collaboration is the key when designing learning opportunities for students. By working together the media specialist and the classroom teacher can design integrated lessons that focus on information literacy, use of technology, and literature appreciation.

The school library media specialist should strive to provide reading programs throughout the year that are based upon the recommendations from state agencies. These activities could include family events, book talks, special guests, and the use of various resources online.

When focusing on the integration of information technology it is important to consult the Technology requirements for each grade level as outlined in the Texas Essential Knowledge and Skills documents.

Attention should also be given to the availability of resources for students beyond the school day. This could include extended hours of operation and/ or home access to school supported web resources.

Skill 1.10   Directs and encourages students to read, view, experience, and listen to a variety of fiction and nonfiction resources for personal and informational needs.

State supported agencies serve as a tool for providing reading activities for students as well as suggested reading lists by age.

- The 2x2 list is for ages 2 through second grade.
- The Texas Bluebonnet Award for grades 3- 6 allows students to vote on their favorite book from a select list. To vote, a student must read at least five of the books on the list.
- The Lone Star list is a reading list for grades 6 – 8.
- The Tayshus list is a reading list for high schoolers.

Children's/adolescent literature of the last 50 years has grown to thousands of new titles per year and many tend to the trendy, the authors and publishers being very aware of the market and the social changes affecting their products. Books are selected for libraries because of their social, psychological, and intellectual value. Collections must also contain materials that recognize cultural and ethnic needs. Because so many popular titles, especially in the young adult area, deal with controversial subjects, school library media specialists are faced with juggling the preferences of their student patrons with the need to provide worthwhile literature and maintain intellectual freedom in the face of increasing censorship.

Books of the young child reader teach about his relationships to the world around him and to other people and things in that world. They help him learn how things operate and how to overcome his fears. Like the still popular fairy tales of previous centuries, some of today's popular children's books are fantasies or allegories, such as Robert O'Brien's *Mrs. Frisby and the Rats of NIMH.*

Popular books for preadolescents deal more with establishing relationships with members of the opposite sex and learning to cope with their changing bodies, personalities.

Well-known writers of children's fiction include Betty Byars, Susan Cooper, Shirley Hughes, Sheila Solomon Klass, Elizabeth Speare, Gary K. Wolf, and Lawrence Yep. Children's poets include Nancy Larrick, Maurice Sendak, and Sol Silverstein.

Fiction writers popular with young adolescents include Judy Blume, Alice Childress, Beverly Cleary, Roald Dahl, Virginia Hamilton, Kathryn Lasky, Lois Lowry, Robin McKinley, Katherine Peterson, Teresa Tomlinson, and Bill Wallace.

Bookseller John Newbery was the first to publish literature for children on any scale in the second half of 18th century England, the great outpouring of children's literature came 100 years later in the Victorian Age. Novels such as Charles Dickens' *Oliver Twist*, Robert Louis Stevenson's *Treasure Island*, and Rudyard Kipling's *Jungle Book*, though not written for children alone, have become classics in children's literature. These books not only helped them understand the world they lived in but satisfied their sense of adventure.

The Newberry Award was created in honor of John Newberry in 1922. This award is presented to an author of the most notable children's or young adult work of fiction.

Newberry awarded books for the past fifteen years include:
   2007 - *The Higher Power of Lucky* written by Susan Patron, illustrated by Matt Phelan
   2006- *Criss Cross* by Lynne Rae Perkins
   2005 - *Kira-Kira* by Cynthia Kadohata
   2004 - *The Tale of Despereaux: Being the Story of a Mouse, a Princess, Some Soup, and a Spool of Thread* by Kate DiCamillo, illustrated by Timothy Basil Ering
   2003- *Crispin: The Cross of Lead* by Avi
   2002 - *A Single Shard* by Linda Sue Park
   2001 - *A Year Down Yonder* by by Richard Peck
   2000 - *Bud, Not Buddy* by Christopher Paul Curtis
   1999 - *Holes* by Louis Sachar
   1998 - *Out of the Dust* by Karen Hesse
   1997 - *The View from Saturday* by E.L. Konigsburg
   1996 - *The Midwife's Apprentice* by Karen Cushman
   1995 - *Walk Two Moons* by Sharon Creech
   1994 - *The Giver* by Lois Lowry

Books for younger children generally include picture books. Notable illustrators of children's books include Marcia Brown, Leo and Diane Dillon, Barbara Dooney, Nonny Hogrogian, David Macaulay, Emily Arnold McCully, Allen Say, Maurice Sendak, Chris Van Allsburg, and David Wiesner.

Each year an outstanding illustrator of a children's book is honored for their outstanding work by being presented with the Caldecott Medal. This award was created in honor of Randolph Caldecott and is distributed annually by the *Association for Library Service for Children.* It was first presented in 1938.

Award winners for the past fifteen years include:
2007 - *Flotsam* by David Wiesner
2006 - *The Hello, Goodbye Window* illustrated by Chris Raschka and written by Norton Juster
2005 - *Kitten's First Full Moon* by Kevin Henkes
2004 - *The Man Who Walked Between the Towers* by Mordicai Gerstein
2003 - *My Friend Rabbit* by Eric Rohmann
2002 - *The Three Pigs* by David Wiesner
2001 - *So You Want to Be President?* Illustrated by David Small, written by Judith St. George
2000 - *Had a Little Overcoat* Simms Taback
1999 - **Snowflake Bentley**, Illustrated by Mary Azarian, text by Jacqueline Briggs Martin
1998 - *Rapunzel* by Paul O. Zelinsky
1997 - *Golem* by David Wisniewski
1996 - *Officer Buckle and Gloria* by Peggy Rathmann
1995 - *Smoky Night*, illustrated by David Diaz; text: Eve Bunting
1994 - *Grandfather's Journey* by Allen Say; text: edited by Walter Lorraine
1993 - *Mirette on the High Wire* by Emily Arnold McCully

Other awards have come about in recent years.
The *Coretta Scott King Award* is presented to outstanding African Americans authors and illustrators for their outstanding educational contributions.

The Laura Ingalls Wilder award honors an author or illustrator whose books have made a significant and lasting contribution to literature for children. The books must be published in the United States.

COMPETENCY 2   (LIBRARY ENVIRONMENT) THE SCHOOL LIBRARIAN ESTABLISHES A LIBRARY ENVIRONMENT THAT ENABLES AND ENCOURAGES ALL MEMBERS OF THE LEARNING COMMUNITY TO EXPLORE AND MEET THEIR INFORMATION NEEDS.

Skill 2.1   Understands principles of exemplary library design as defined by state and federal guidelines for a simultaneous-use facility for individuals, small groups, and classes.

The specifics of design spatial arrangement of a library media center should support and promote a lively media program and reflect the school's vision for learning. Attention needs to be given to the types and quantities of resources and services provided. New school design should place the media center in a central location, easily accessible to all academic areas. Within the center itself the following spatial arrangement factors should be addressed.

1.   A large central area for reading, listening, viewing, and computing, which has ready access to materials and equipment. AASL/AECT guidelines recommend that this main seating area be 25% - 75% of the total square footage allocation, depending on program requirements. 40 square feet should be allotted per student user. Within this area or peripheral to it should be smaller areas that provide for independent study or accommodate students with physical impairments. Seating should be adequate to accommodate the number of users during peak hours. SAC guidelines recommend floor space and seating to accommodate 10% of the student body, but the media center should not be expected to seat fewer than 40 or more than 100 students at one time.

2.   Areas for small or medium-sized group activities. These areas may be acoustically special spaces adjacent to the central seating area or conference rooms, computer labs, or storytelling space. AASL/AECT recommends 1 - 3 areas or approximately 150 square feet with ample electrical outlets, good lighting and acoustics, and a wall screen.

3.   Space to house and display the collection. Materials that can be circulated outside the center should be easily accessible from the main seating area. Index tools should be highly visible and in the immediate proximity to the collections they index. A supervised circulation desk with easy access to non-circulable databases (periodicals, CD- ROM disks, microform, and videotape collections) should be close to the center's main entrance. AASL/AECT recommends 400 square feet minimum for stacks with an additional 200 foot allowance per 500 additional students.

4.   A reference materials area within or adjacent to the central seating area. The recommended area allowance is part of the total allotted for the stacks.

5. Space for a professional collection and work area where the faculty and media professionals can work privately. This area should be approximately 1 square foot per student.

6. Administrative offices, with areas for resource and equipment processing, materials duplication, and business materials storage. An area no smaller than 200 square feet should be available for offices alone and double that area if in-house processing is done.

7. Equipment storage and circulation area close to administrative offices and with access to outside corridor. Space for maintenance and repair is optional depending on available staff to attend to these duties. This space should be no less than 400 square feet for storage with another 150 square feet if repair facilities are necessary.

8. A media production area with space and equipment for production of audio and videotaping, graphics design, photography, computer programming, and photocopying. (In some secondary schools, a dark room is included. Other schools with commercial photography classes and a full photography lab may seek services through the photography teacher.) This area may be as small as 50 square feet or as large as 700 square feet in a school with 500 students depending on the amount of equipment required to suit media production needs; in a school with 1000 or more students at least 700-900 square feet should be allotted for media production.

9. A television production studio for formal TV production class instruction and preparing special programming. Space for distribution of closed circuit programs and satellite transmissions should also be provided. A 1600 square foot studio (preferably 40' x 40' x 15') should be available whenever television classes are taught or studio videotaping is a program priority. AASL/AECT guidelines allow alternatives: studio space available at district for the use of students or mini-studios/portable videotape units where videotaping is done on a small scale.

10. Recommended, but optional in many schools, is a large multi-purpose room adjacent to the media center for use as a lecture hall or meeting room. AASL/AECT recommends that this room be 700-900 square feet in a school with 500 student school (i.e. classroom size) or 900-1200 square feet in a school with 1000 students. This room should be equipped for making all types of media presentations.

11. A network / server head-end area that would house network services, telephone equipment, and video distribution equipment for the entire building. The space should be from 450- 800 square feet. Equipment for this room may include network server, routers switches, telephone patch panel, cabling, and wireless devices.

12. Network access and power outlets should be available throughout the entire media center to accommodate circulation search stations, student work stations and other electronic devices.

Skill 2.2   Develops and maintains a flexible, functional, and barrier-free library facility that is safe, secure, and age-appropriate.

There are important design elements to consider when renovating or building new facilities.

1.   Traffic flow should provide easy, logical access to all spaces.
2.   A realistic assessment of security needs will provide for material detection systems, alarms or locks to protect electronic equipment, and convenient placement of communications devices.
3.   Proper placement of electrical outlets, fire extinguishers, smoke detectors, and thermostats ensures safety for users and convenience for the staff.
4.   Provision must be made for the physically impaired to have barrier-free access to the center and its resources.
5.   All areas requiring supervision should be readily visible from other areas of the center.
6.   There should be a carefully planned relationship of spaces used for supporting activities and services.

See Skill 2.1 for additional guidelines.

Skill 2.3   Uses space effectively in the school library (e.g., for displays of student-produced, faculty-produced, and community-produced materials and collections).

The media center should be an inviting place for all patrons. The space should be attractive and have displays containing products from various populations within the learning community. *School Library Programs: Standards and Guidelines for Texas* expresses that exemplary media centers provide a variety of display areas to house these projects.

Skill 2.4   Promotes equitable access to resources and information during and beyond the instructional day and school year.

Resource sharing is a way of

1.   Providing a broader information base to enable users to find and access the resources that provide the needed information.
2.   Reducing or containing media center budgets.
3.   Establishing cooperation with other resource providers that encourage mutual planning and standardization of control.

Resource sharing systems:

1.   Interlibrary loan. The advent of computer databases has simplified the process of locating sources in other libraries.

Local public library collections can be accessed from terminals in the media center. Physical access depends on going to the branch where the material is housed.

2. Networking systems.

    Sharing information has become even easier with the use of network services. Files can be shared and accessed from room to room, school to school and city to city. Resources can be shared within a small geographic location such as a school by the use of a local area network or LAN. A wide area network or WAN is used to communicate over a larger area such as a school district or city.

    a. E-mail allows educators to communicate across the state.

    b. On-line services (Internet providers) offer access to a specific menu of locations. Monthly fees and/or time charges must be budgeted.

    c. Individual city or county network systems. These are community sponsored networks, often part of the public library system, which provides Internet access for the price of a local phone call. A time limit usually confines an individual search to allow more users access.

    d. On-line continuing education programs offer courses/ degrees through at-home study. Large school districts provide lessons for homebound students or home school advocates.

    e. Bulletin boards allow individuals or groups to converse electronically with persons in another place.

3. Telecommunications. Using telephone and television as the media for communication, telecommunications is used primarily for distance learning. Universities or networks of universities (University of South Carolina and a consortium in North Carolina) provide workshops, conferences, and college credit courses for educators as well as courses for senior high school students in subjects that could not generate adequate class counts in their home schools. Large school districts offer broadcast programming for homebound/home school students.

    The advantage is that students are provided with a phone number so they can interact with the instructors or information providers.

Skill 2.5   Creates a learning environment in which the diversity of groups and the uniqueness of individuals are recognized and appreciated.

The mission of a school library media program should be to provide access to information to all students and staff. Information needs to be provided in a wide array of formats, topics, and levels to meet the needs of a diverse population.

The collection should include tools to assist students with both physical and learning impairments, materials for gifted students and a variety of topics to cover student's interests.

It is important to involve students in decisions concerning the media program. Including them in the library advisory committee and involving the student council can be good avenues for gaining student support. When students contribute to the development of a library media program they take ownership of their learning.

The key factor in creating an environment conducive to learning is the expertise of the library media specialist. They are the expert regarding all aspects of information literacy. They have the responsibility of not only providing a quality collection of resources, but in teaching staff and students the processes they need to become information literate themselves. The school library media specialist must teach them how to access, evaluate, and use information. This includes teaching staff and students how to use the tools on hand to facilitate the process.

Skill 2.6 Provides access to library resources and facilities through open, flexible scheduling for classes, small groups, and individuals.

The mission of the school library media center is to provide physical and intellectual access to information at the point of need. This is best accomplished through open and flexibly scheduled classes. A flexible schedule promotes learning at the point of need and provides the media specialist with opportunities to work collaboratively with both staff and students.

The issue of flexible access is especially distressing to elementary school library media specialists who are placed in the "related arts wheel, " providing planning time for art, music, and physical education teachers. "Closed" or rigid scheduling, i.e. scheduling classes to meet regularly for instruction in the library, prohibits the implementation of the integrated program philosophy essential to the principles of intellectual freedom.

The AASL Position Statement on Flexible Scheduling asserts that schools must adopt a philosophy of full integration of library media into the total educational program. This integration assures a partnership of students, teachers, and school library media specialists in the use of readily accessible materials and services when they are appropriate to the classroom curriculum

All parties in the school community - teachers, principal, district administration, and school board - must share the responsibility for contributing to flexible access.

Research on the validity of flexible access reinforces the need for cooperative planning with teachers, an objective that cannot be met if the school library media specialist has no time for the required planning sessions. Rigid scheduling denies students the freedom to come to the library during the school day for pleasurable reading and self-motivated inquiry activities vital to the development of critical thinking, problem solving, and exploratory skills. Without flexible access, the library becomes just another self-contained classroom.

DOMAIN II.   PROGRAM MANAGEMENT,
                             LEADERSHIP,
                             AND CONNECTIONS TO THE
                             COMMUNITY

COMPETENCY 3   **(LIBRARY PROGRAM MANAGEMENT) THE SCHOOL LIBRARIAN UNDERSTANDS LIBRARY PROGRAM MANAGEMENT AND ACQUIRES, ORGANIZES, AND MANAGES RESOURCES.**

Skill 3.1   **Uses effective decision making (e.g., synthesizing information from a variety of sources) to develop and maintain an exemplary library program.**

An exemplary library program is one that is constantly striving to improve. By evaluating the school library media program the media specialist can identify strengths and weaknesses of the existing program. From the information gleaned from the evaluations program improvements can be made.

Evaluation requires standards, the conditions that should exist if the program is to be judged successful. Some of these standards may already be determined by national or state guidelines that districts administrators have agreed to maintain. School libraries in Texas rely upon a comprehensive evaluation guide that provides specific guidelines for gathering data as well as the formulas for calculating results available linked to the *School Library Programs: Standards and Guidelines for Texas* document. This process is divided into two main categories: Output and Evidence-based measures.

Output measures provide quantitative data regarding the school library media program. This type of data can measure how frequently services and resources are utilized. This process divides library requests into that of planning requests and resource requests. There are specific data collection forms and formals for calculating information

Evidences-based measures work with qualitative data, standards designed to express essentially the measured criteria as quantitative without exact numerical amounts. With this method, students and staff complete questionnaires or are interviewed to gain insight into attitudes, knowledge, behaviors and knowledge of skills. To measure this form of data a rubric is created that outlines specific indicators to determine the level of success.

Once the data is collected and analyzed the plan for improvement is created. The process of evaluation is continuous. School library media specialists strive to provide an outstanding program. As new goals are adopted they must be evaluated and adjusted to determine effectiveness and the cycle continues.

Skill 3.2   Develops procedures for the school library program to ensure compliance with Board policies and local, state, and federal laws.

A policy is the written statement of principle in which the policy-making agency guarantees a management practice or course of action that is expedient and consistent. A procedure is the course of action taken to execute the policy. In government, legislation is policy and law enforcement is procedure.

Educational policy makers include the Congress and state legislatures, state and local school boards, national library media organizations, and school library media program managers. Policies adopted at the local level must support district school board policies and state laws.

Regulations concerning certification, state budget allocations, and standards for selecting and approving state-adopted instructional materials are developed at the state level.

Matters such as collection development and responding to challenges of materials are usually set at district level.

Local issues such as hours of operation, circulation of materials and equipment, and personnel supervision are set by the appropriate school policy makers for library media.

Procedures for administering district and state policies are usually determined by usual practice or local precedence.

Procedures for specific administration tasks such as determining budget categories, expending funds, maintaining collection size and so many others should be clearly stated in a school library media procedures manual.

There are two basic sources for district policies, school board rules and the procedures manual from district media services offices. Information provided in these documents should be reviewed before any school level planning is done.

It is also necessary to know which policies and procedures are the responsibility of the district and which ones are the responsibility of the school. For example, school boards are charged with the responsibility to set propriety standards for instructional material selection. However, school boards do not select the texts or library books for individual schools. Procedures for implementing propriety standards are determined at each school site based on the needs of its students.

School boards may set policy for a challenge and identify a procedure for its sequential investigation. The school library media specialist as a defender of intellectual freedom and a trained educator should have the latitude to recommend and purchase quality materials. She should also be prepared to substantiate those purchases in terms of readability, social appropriateness, and artistic quality.

Operational procedures change from district-to-district. Some counties have centralized reprographics facilities; therefore, district policies are set for reproduction of materials that comply with copyright laws and district procedures for formatting, according to the type of equipment used, are spelled out in a printed manual which should be available at all school sites.
Some counties have centralized materials processing so that classification and cataloging procedures are administered at the county level.

It is always preferable to develop local policies and procedures with the aid of a library advisory committee.

Participants	Role
Administrator	clarifies school vision and goals.
Media specialist	identifies factors such as time, personnel, resources, and budget that affect school goals.
Teacher	identifies media center resources and services that correlate with instruction.
Student	identifies materials and activities that fulfill learning needs.
Parents (Optional)	identify avenues of communication with parents and community.

Once the advisory committee has formulated acceptable policies and procedures, the district director and/or directors of elementary and secondary instruction should review and provide input before adoption.

Constant evaluation is necessary to determine the effectiveness of a school library media procedures manual. Things to consider during the evaluation process are:
- Do the procedures outline the most efficient methods for completing the task?
- Do the policies and procedures reflect the principles of the library profession with regards to intellectual freedom, copyright, and the rights of all users?
- Do the policies and procedures promote and enhance student learning?

- Do the policies and procedures provide equitable access to resources?
- Do the policies and procedures provide maximum access to resources?
- Do the policies and procedures promote responsible use of resources?
- Do the policies and procedures comply with national, state, and local guidelines?

Skill 3.3   Uses effective strategies and techniques for systematically performing fiscal library management operations (e.g., record keeping, budgeting, purchasing, grant writing).

In preparation for constructing the budget for the school library media center, the school media professionals need to consider

1.   The standards set by state departments of education, local school boards, and regional accreditation associations. Changes in standards sometimes necessitate changes in local budget planning.
2.   The sources of funds that support the media center program.
3.   The prioritized list of program goals and the cost of meeting these goals.

Determining the relationship between program goals and funding involve the study of

1.   Past inventories and projections of future needs.
2.   Quantitative and qualitative collection standards at all levels.
3.   School and district curriculum plans.
4.   Community needs.
5.   Fiscal deadlines.

Exemplary school library media programs focus on a 5-year plan for implementing and evaluating their budget.

AASL/AECT provides guidelines for four factors in calculating the budget for the print and non-print collection: variation in student population, attrition by weeding, attrition by date, and attrition by loss. A formula for an estimated budget is then calculated based on points established for each of these factors. The estimation for replacement is figured on a base number of collection items required regardless of school size. The minimum collection standard is determined by the state or regional accreditation requirements.

Another method of estimating a budget for the print collection is based on the types of materials needed: replacement books, periodicals, books for growth and expansion, and reference books.

An acceptable library media program would use the following formula when considering the purchase of print resources:

(1.00 X the number of students) x   the average replacement cost of a book as reported yearly in the School Library Journal.

There are various formulas that can be used to assist with determining the amount of funded needed to purchase periodicals, equipment and technology resources.

Having considered all factors, the budget process should parallel budget plans to the program goals and objectives. To achieve this correlation the process should follow these steps.

1.	Communicate program and budget considerations to administration, faculty, students and community groups, allowing sufficient time for input from all groups.
2.	Work with representatives from all groups to finalize short- range objectives and review long-range goals for use of funds.
3.	Build a system of flexible encumbrance and transferal of funds as changes in needs occur.
4.	As part of the program promotion, communicate budgetary concerns to all interested parties.

Unlike public libraries, school library media centers are not usually the recipients of endowments or private gifts. School library media centers receive money from local and state tax dollars. The major portion of the funds comes from district allotments for instructional materials or capital outlay that are regulated by the state. Schools that have accreditation must adhere to regional guidelines that assure that accreditation. The funding formulas specifically used for school library media budgets vary from district to district but basically comply with the following regulations.

State:
1.	Local operation. School library media centers funds are generally allocated from the district operating budget. The funds may be administered at the district or school level according to a per capita figure, adequate to meet operation costs and contractual obligations.
2.	Regional guidelines. SAC produces an expenditures requirement based on student body size, allowing a school to average expenditures over a three-year period in which averaged expenditures do not fall below the standard.
3.	State funds provided by special legislation. Most special funds have been in the form of block grants. Block grants are funds earmarked for a specific purpose. Schools generally must apply for such funds. One example is the technology block grants that have appeared in recent years. These grants have provided funds for retrofitting schools to create local area networks, wide-area networks, and telecommunications services.

Federal:
1.   Block grants included in federal education acts (4.6.3). Awarded to states or specific districts, these grants are limited in scope and time. They must be applied for on a competitive basis and renewal depends on the recipient's ability to prove that grant objectives have been met.

2.   Current federal funds are earmarked for innovative technologies not operating costs.

In addition to official funding sources, there are other forms of assistance from the community that should be reflected in the budget plan. Because this assistance is in the form of service rather than real dollars, estimated values must be determined. Some community assistance includes
1.   Partnerships with local businesses. Free wiring from cable television companies, guest speakers, distance learning opportunities, and workshops in new technologies are just a few possible services.
2.   Education support groups. The education committee of the local chamber of commerce, a private education economic council, or parent associations may conduct fund-raisers or offer mini-grants.
3.   Corporate grants. Many large companies provide grants for specific topics such as technology, science, math and reading. The grant may involve providing equipment or funds to be used for a specific purpose.

Once funding has been provided the school library media specialist works closely with school bookkeepers and district personnel to spend the funds promptly to acquire resources. It is important that the school library media specialist understands the process for bidding and purchasing under state contract to receive the best prices possible.

When the materials begin to arrive it is necessary to record basic information as part of the inventory process.

Skill 3.4   Manages and maintains facilities and resources (e.g., scheduling, circulation, inventory, repair, reporting).

Schools should strive to provide open, flexible access to media center resources. Since students do not come at regular intervals it is important for the school library media specialist to continuously evaluate student use of resources. The information gathered by this report can then be shared with the teacher to make sure they are maximizing their use of the media resources.

To alleviate confusion regarding the borrowing of resources, a school library must have circulation policies and procedures in place. Circulation policies and procedures should be flexible to allow ready access and secure to protect borrowers' rights of confidentiality.

The components of circulation procedures:
1.   Circulation system. Most circulation systems are automated, this system should
        a.   Be simple to use for convenience of staff as well as to save time for borrowers.
        b.   Provide for the loan and retrieval of print and non-print materials and equipment.
        c.   Facilitate the collection of circulation statistics.

2.   Rules governing circulation.
        a.   Length of loan period.
        b.   Process for handling overdues.
        c.   Limitations.
                - Number of items circulable to individual borrower.
                - Overnight loan for special items (vertical file materials, reference books, audio-visual materials or equipment).
                - Reserve collections.

3.   Rules governing fines for damages or lost materials.

4.   Security provisions.
        a.   Theft detection devices on print and non-print media.
        b.   Straps or lock-downs on equipment transported by cart.

Materials in the media center become worn with continuous use. It is necessary to have a plan in place that will allow the repairing of damaged books or broken equipment. Print resources may need torn pages mended or bindings reattached. Equipment may require the expertise of a technician. For either case, a process for notifying the media specialists when problems occur should be in place.

Inventory is the process of verifying the collection holdings and assessing the collection's physical condition. Its purposes are

1.   To indicate lost or missing materials. Identify items for replacement.
2.   To reveal strengths and weaknesses in collection. Inventory helps identify areas where numbers of materials do not reflect need.
3.   To identify materials needing repair. Periodic preventive maintenance can save major repair or replacement cost.
4.   To shape the process of weeding. Outdated and damaged or worn materials would be removed to maintain the integrity of the collection's reputation.

Procedures:

1. Specify when inventory will be conducted. Most schools conduct inventories at the end of the school year. Many districts require inventory statistics be turned into the school or district supervisors before media staff vacations.
2. Determine who will conduct inventory. Personnel availability will determine whether inventory will be conducted by professionals, support staff, or some combination, during school hours or during closed time.

3. Examine each item and match it to the holding records. Pull items for repair.
4. Tabulate results and record on forms required by the school or district.

Skill 3.5   Supervises students and implements programs to manage and evaluate human resources.

The American Association of School Librarians (AASL) recommends that a school library media center by a licensed school library media specialist with a Master's degree from an American Library Association (ALA) or National Council for the Accreditation of Teacher Education (NCATE) accredited educational program and qualified support staff.

Professional responsibilities and activities are those outlined in the performance indicators throughout Competency 4. The school library media specialist has responsibility for developing program goals, collection development, budget management, consultation with teachers in using existing resources or producing new materials, provision for student instruction and staff development, and overseeing the paraprofessional and nonprofessional staffs.

The paraprofessional is a person qualified for a special area of media such as graphics, photography, instructional television, electronics, media production, or computer technology. Often called a media or technical assistant, this person has training in his specialty and some education training but does not have a bachelor's degree in library or information sciences. The media or technical assistant may have an AA or BA/BS degree in his/ her specialty. Some community colleges offer certificates in Library Assistantship.

The paraprofessional's responsibilities are in the areas of production, maintenance, and special services to students and teachers. Some of the duties might include

1. Working with teachers in the design and production of media for classroom instruction.
2. Creating promotional materials and preparing special need media (video yearbook, audio or videotape duplication, preparation of materials for faculty meetings and staff development activities).
3. Operating and maintaining production equipment (laminator, audio and video devices).
4. Maintaining computers and peripherals.
5. Evaluating media and equipment collection and recommending purchases.
6. Developing ways to use existing and emerging technologies.
7. Assisting teachers and students in locating and using media and equipment.
8. Repairing or making provisions for repair of materials and equipment.
9. Circulating equipment.
10. Maintaining records on circulation, maintenance, and repair of media and equipment.

The non-professional staff assumes responsibility for operational procedures (clerical, secretarial, technical, maintenance) that relieve the school library professional and paraprofessional of routine tasks so they can better perform their responsibilities.

Some specific nonprofessional activities:

1. Conducting accounting and bookkeeping procedures.
2. Unpacking, processing and shelving new materials.
3. Processing correspondences, records, manuals, etc.
4. Circulating materials and equipment.
5. Assisting with materials production.
6. Assisting with maintenance and repair of materials and equipment.
7. Handling accounting procedures.
8. Assisting with inventory.
9. Assisting with services provided by electronic and computer equipment.

The diversity of user needs, school enrollments, and school/district support services are some factors that affect staff size. Some of the duties of different levels of staff persons overlap and differ only in the amount of decision-making and accountability.

If the school places a high priority on an efficient library media center program, there should be a minimum of two full-time professionals, one paraprofessional and two nonprofessionals, one to function as an office manager and one as a technical assistant.

However, ALA and NEA standards for School Media Programs recommended two support staff for each specialist in any school with under 2000 enrollment. SAC Standards recommend that in a school with two specialists on staff, two paraprofessionals may be hired in lieu of an additional professional. Unfortunately, when schools are looking to save money, it is generally the support staff which is sacrificed.

When the support staff is reduced, the professional must assume operational duties which detract from his professional responsibilities. Volunteers can help with circulation and supplemental tasks that reflect their unique talents and experiences, but they should never be used as substitutes for paid clerical and technical staff. Student assistants, like volunteers, may be trained to assist the media specialist but should not be given duties that are the responsibilities of paid nonprofessionals. They might assist with production of materials, maintenance of the decoration and physical appearance of the center, instruction in materials location, use of electronic/computer databases, use or maintenance of equipment and shelving books and periodicals. It is recommended that student aides be given course credit or certificates of achievement to reward them for their services.

Most untrained support staff will need to be trained on the job.

1. Using the district's job description and evaluation instrument for the particular position, prioritize the skills in order from greatest to least immediacy.
2. Determine the already mastered skills by observing performance.
3. Plan a systematic training of remaining skills to be addressed one at a time.

Supervision of media professionals is the responsibility of an administrator. Supervision of support staff is the responsibility of the head library media specialist (if that position is administrative) or of an administrator with input from the media specialist. Periodic oral evaluations and annual written evaluations using the appropriate instrument should be conducted for each media staff member. These evaluations should result in suggestions for training or personal development.

Skill 3.6   Collaborates with faculty to evaluate (e.g., select, weed) library resources that support the curriculum and leisure reading.

A collection of resources that closely ties the school's instructional program as well as the developmental and cultural needs of students is crucial to the school library media program.

To ensure the collection meets student needs there are steps the media specialist can take:
1. Stay abreast of changes in curriculum as well as the types of resources needed to meet those needs.
2. Work closely with teachers to determine resources needed.
3. Work closely with staff to determine policies and procedures.
4. Develop specific processes for evaluating and updating the collection.
5. Have access to up-to-date collection monitoring and evaluation tools and reviewing resources.
6. Support the circulation of resources by sharing information with teachers and allowing them to preview new resources as well as take part in the selection process.

A collection that is current and meets the needs of staff and students requires weeding or the discarding of worn or outdated materials. There are many resources that provide assistance with weeding procedures. A few things to take into consideration when reviewing your collection for weeding are:
1. Weeding should be an ongoing process.
2. Criteria for weeding is sometimes subjective, but can be based on the following categories:

USE – Look for materials not circulated regularly

WEAR – torn, stained, ripped materials may need to be ordered or let go

SUBJECT – the information in the resource is outdated or no longer valid or has been replaced by a newer, updated version of the material

AVAILABLE ELSEWHERE – If the material is readily available electronically or through another resource and is not often used, it may be worth discarding

A popular acronym to consider when weeding is MUSTIE.
* Misleading
* Ugly
* Superseded
* Trivial
* Irrelevant
* Elsewhere

Consider, when weeding, extenuating circumstances that might warrant the saving of materials, such as works by local authors, memorial gifts, or local histories.

Here are the suggested weeding procedures for each Dewey level:
- 000 – encyclopedias every five years, other materials no more than eight years
- 100 – five to eight years
- 200 – can be high turnover with religious books – keep current
- 300 – almanacs replace every two years, keep political information current
- 400 – check for wear and tear frequently
- 500 -- continuously update to make sure scientific information is current
- 600 -- continuously update medical information as older information can be misleading or dangerous
- 700 – keep until worn
- 800 – keep until worn
- 900 – weed about every two years
- Biography – keep most current or best written titles
- Adult fiction – weed for multiple copies, keep those in best shape and that have the most literary value
- Young-adult and children's fiction – same as adult fiction
- Reference – weed for currency and accuracy

Skill 3.7   Designs and implements acceptable use policies for current and emerging technologies.

With ever emerging technologies, schools and districts need to ensure the resources available are used for educational purposes. It is necessary to outline both appropriate and inappropriate behaviors that concern these resources.

Districts need to create an acceptable use policy. This provides guidelines for the use of the school or district's electronic resources and the consequences that occur if the resources are not used properly.

When creating the document it is important to include: key intranet network policy issues: use of email, bulletin board postings, abuse of network resources, and netiquette.

Guidelines for personal use of the district's Internet resources should be listed in the policy as well as Web publishing guidelines for maintaining school and teacher web pages.

Once the document is created, staff and students must be trained to understand what the guidelines are and consequences that could result if an infringement occurs.

Skill 3.8 Monitors, assesses, and employs existing and emerging technologies for management applications.

Automated circulation systems have made managing resources easier and faster than ever before. Using an automated system allows the media specialist to quickly examine circulation statistics, frequency of use, and flag records of items that may need weeding.

To prepare to convert to an automated library management system there are three main categories that must be considered. The first is the budget, next includes the technical considerations needed for automation and the other is the data conversion.

The options available during the conversion process are often determined by the funds available. Necessary purchases would include the software, a barcode scanner for checkout, necessary hardware upgrades, and technical support. Other options could include a web based searching option for home use and paying other companies to convert records. It is good to have a well-defined plan before beginning the process. When in doubt, take small steps and increase as time and money allows.

Technical considerations fall into the software, hardware and infrastructure categories. When selecting software for library management, check local or state recommendations before making any decisions. The platform should match the computer systems most prevalent in your district. If your school is predominantly MAC based then use a MAC platform; if Windows, use Windows. Before purchasing the software, make sure the computers in the school will support the requirements of the software and that the network infrastructure is in place to provide maximum access. District technical support staff should be able to assist with these decisions. It will be important to purchase or make sure that technical support is provided for the automation software manufacturer. This may involve an extra expense, but will be money well spent especially during the initial setup phase.

After the technical requirements are in place, it is time to begin the data conversion process. Transferring the current card catalog into electronic format can be a daunting job. It helps first to thoroughly weed the collection. By weeding, time is saved by not converting titles that will be discarded.

The actual conversion of information to electronic format will be the most time consuming task. Options include inputting the data onsite or hiring a company to convert the shelflist to electronic format. Budget is generally the biggest consideration. If the choice is to convert onsite a wise investment would be the purchase of MARC CD-ROMS. This will make the process move much faster. There are companies who will convert the shelflist to MARC format for a rather minimal charge considering the time it takes to enter everything by hand. Explore the possibilities of utilizing such services and determine the impact on the automation budget.

Once the shelflist has been converted to electronic format, books must be barcoded. This generally involves printing barcode stickers and placing them on each and every book. Volunteers and student helpers can make this process move quickly.

Next, all patrons need to be added into the system. This can often be conducted by importing data from the school's attendance management system. If not, information will need to be keyed in by hand.

Once all of the information is in then the school library media specialist needs to set up basic information such as checkout limits, the amount of time a book can be checked out, and other basic housekeeping information.

The conversion to an automated system is a lot of work, but the benefits far outweigh the time it would take to complete the process.

Skill 3.9 Uses effective planning, time management, and organization of work to maximize attainment of district and campus goals.

Proper planning is essential to the success of any school library media program. The planning process will take determination, but a quality media program is of great benefit to any school.

For the planning process to be successful, it must have the support of your principal. Other key people within your school must be included such as teachers, school support staff, parents, and students. This group of individuals would become part of a school library planning committee sometimes known as the Media Advisory Committee (MAC) or Media and Technology Advisory Committee (MTAC). Utilizing such a committee approach is reflective of site-based management. In site-based management decisions are made by a group of stakeholders or committee rather than being left to the discretion of one person.

One of the first things the planning committee must do is develop a mission statement that defines the core purpose of the school library media program.

The mission statement must become the main focus from which all goals are formed and decisions are made.

The mission of any organization, business, or educational institution should evolve from the needs and expectations of its customers. In the case of the school library media center, its mission must parallel the school's mission and attend to the users' needs for resources and services.

The school library media program should examine school and student characteristics.

School:

1.   The mission of the school library media center should reflect and be in harmony with the stated school mission.
2.   The program's mission should reflect the curricular direction of the school: academic, vocational, compensatory.
3.   The mission should reflect the willingness of the administration and faculty to support the program.

Student:

1.   The mission is influenced by pupil demographics: age, achievement and ability levels, reading levels, and learning styles.
2.   The mission may indicate the students' interest in self- directed learning and exploratory reading.
3.   The mission reflects support from parents and community groups.

Once a mission has been defined, it is important to assess the current status of the program and see how closely it follows that mission. Gathering this information is essential to the formation of effective goals and objectives.

It is important to note that evaluation is an ongoing process. It must occur prior to determining goals and objectives and on a regular basis thereafter to ensure they are being met.

A wide variety of evaluation criteria may be used. The criteria may be

1.   Diagnostic.   These are standards based on conditions existing in programs that have already been judged excellent.
2.   Projective. These standards are guidelines for conditions as they ought to be ideally.
3.   Quantitative. These standards require numerical measurement.
4.   Qualitative. These standards are designed to express essentially the measured criteria as quantitative without exact numerical amounts.

Most school library media programs evaluations have been diagnostic or qualitative. Diagnostic prescriptions alone make no allowances for specific conditions in given schools and are often interpreted too liberally; qualitative prescriptions alone are difficult to measure or sustain. Projective standards are usually broad national guidelines which serve best as long-range goals. Preferably, a program evaluation, utilizing a combination of quantitative and qualitative standards, produces results that can lead to modified objectives. Statistics to substantiate quantitative standards can be derived from:

1.   Usage statistics from automated circulation systems. These indicate frequency of materials use.
2.   Inventory figures. Resource turnover, loss and damage, and missing materials statistics indicate extent of use. Total materials count can substantiate materials per student criteria.
3.   Individual circulation logs. Such logs indicate the frequency of patron use of library materials and the types of materials used.
4.   Class scheduling log. Depending on the amount of data acquired when a visit is scheduled, several facts can be determined: proportion of staff and student body using materials and services; the frequency of use of specific resources or services; the age levels of users; specific subgroups being served; and subject matter preferences.

Evidence of meeting qualitative standards can be derived from
1.   Lesson plans. Careful planning will reveal the frequency of use of resources and specific classroom objectives planned cooperatively with faculty. The plan should also specify the effectiveness with which the students achieved the lesson objectives.
2.   Personnel evaluations. Most districts have formative and/or summative evaluations for the professional/para- professional/non-professional staff. Student aides should receive educational credit for their services hours. Completion of specific skills and termination grades can provide both quantitative and qualitative data.
3.   Surveys. A systematic written evaluation should be conducted annually to obtain input from students, teachers, and parents on the success of program objectives.
4.   Conferences / Library Advisory Committee meetings. Faculty members' and students' comments can provide qualitative assessment of the value of the materials and services provided.
5.   Criterion-referenced or teacher made tests. These assessments can be used to evaluate student effectiveness in acquiring information skills or content area skills.

The purposes of evaluation are to determine if all aspects of planning and implementation have been successfully accomplished. If evaluation shows unsuccessful outcomes, then the program must be modified. Successful outcomes can be used to confirm program objectives and to promote the media center programs.

Some strategies for the use of program evaluation include

1.   To produce an annual report to be included in the school's annual report to parents or other publications for circulation in the community.
2.   To review and modify long-range goals and plan immediate changes in short-range goals.
3.   To lobby for budgetary or personnel support.
4.   To solicit assistance from faculty and administration in making curricular or instructional changes to maximize use of media center materials, equipment, and services.
5.   To plan greater involvement of students in academic and personal use of media center materials and services.

There is now so much outstanding resource material and the technology to easily identify these resources that the task can be managed by following a few simple steps.

1.   Rely on the information provided in this guide's resource list. If your school or district's professional library does not contain these resources, visit the public library in the nearest large city or a university library where information sciences are taught.
2.   Give your school media program a close examination before doing your research. Study any written evaluations by media personnel, school improvement committees, library advisory committees, or annual reports. Informally survey a cross-section of students and teachers to gather input about their perceptions of the materials and services that are provided.
3.   Make a list of questions based on the concerns that result from your evaluation. Peruse the questions in Chapter One of *Information Power* to see if there are any pertinent areas that have not yet been addressed.
4.   Do your research.
5   Produce a written evaluation of your school's library media program based on your findings. Submit this evaluation to the principal and plan with her the best way to communicate the information to students, teachers, and parents.
6.   Gather input from all groups to whom your evaluation is presented.
7.   Meet with the Library Media Advisory Committee or equivalent group to formulate program changes. Be sure to include students and parents or lay community members on this committee.
8.   Implement the changes and plan subsequent evaluations.

Once an initial program evaluation has been completed, program goals and objectives may be determined. These goals and objectives help to break down the overall vision into areas that the school feels are most important for the successful operation of a school library media program. Some of these goals may already be determined by national or state guidelines that districts administrators have agreed to maintain. Sometimes, a district operates without a program to guide school library media centers. In that case each school must be responsible not only for setting its own criteria but also for inspiring some district planning.

The first step would be to define major goals. A goal is a broad statement of an intended outcome that reflects the mission of the school library media program that provides direction.

A goal is a long-range plan. Therefore, when planning a school library media program based on an assessment of school and student characteristics, the program planning team should factor in these elements.

A long-range plan should

1. Extend from 3-5 years.
2. Incorporate the goals of the other departments (grade levels or content teams) in the school.
3. Be stated in terms that are non-limiting. The goal should be an achievable aim, not a pipe dream.

Specific goals for school library media centers are outlined in *Information Power: Building Partnerships for Learning.* Key points include:

- providing access to resources and information through integrated activities on a variety of levels
- providing physical access to a wide variety of resources and information from various locations including outside agencies and electronic resources
- assist patrons in locating and evaluating information
- collaborate with teachers and others
- facilitate the lifelong learning process
- build a school library media program that acts as the hub of all learning within the school
- provide resources that embrace differences culturally and socially and support concepts of intellectual freedom

After the major goals have been defined, objectives must be determined. An objective is a specific statement of a measurable result that will occur by a particular time, i.e. it must specify the conditions and criteria to be met effectively. Objectives reflect short- term priorities. Objectives have a specific format. They must contain an action verb and must be measurable. A few of the action verbs often seen in objectives are: discuss, define, compare, identify, explain, and design.

An objective is a short-range plan. A short-range plan should be one part of a longer range plan that is

1. Accomplishable in one year or less.
2. Linked meaningfully in a logical progression to the expressed goal.
3. Flexible, as most objectives must be processed through affected groups before finalization.

In an Olympic year an appropriate example of goals and objectives might be

Goal: To win an Olympic Medal.
Objectives:

1. To increase my speed by .05 seconds per meter by June 30.
2. To double my practice time during the two weeks before the competition begins.
3. To lose 3 lbs. before my weigh-in.

If translated into goals and objectives for library media centers it may read as follows:

Goal: To develop a collection more suited to the academic demands of the curriculum
Objectives:

1. To increase non-fiction collection by 10% in the next school year.
2. To ensure readability levels suited to gifted students for 5% of new selections.

Goal: To provide telecommunications services within three years.
Objectives:

1. To design a model for instructional use in 1996.
2. To plan for equipment and facilities needs in 1997.
3. To implement the model with a control group in 1998.

If a school seeks or wishes to maintain accreditation with the Southern Association of Colleges and Schools (SAC), using that organization's recommendations is an excellent way to set program goals and objectives. Because SAC requires every accredited school to conduct an intensive ten year reevaluation and five year interim reviews, the library media center program planners may wish to coordinate their own study with the SAC's reviews.

With the demands places on a school library media specialist time management is of the utmost importance. Flexible schedules provide a more conducive learning environment for students, but may pose a challenge to the school library media specialist. There are a few helpful things to remember when planning for the day:

- Establish priorities.
- Delegate.
- Minimize interruptions.

To assist the media specialist in determining which areas devour most of the time during the day, keep a time log over the period of a few days. Record each activity and the amount of time it consumes each day. By evaluating the results the media specialist can plan a schedule that minimizes trivial and unimportant time wasters.

COMPETENCY 4   **(LIBRARY PROGRAM LEADERSHIP AND CONNECTIONS TO THE COMMUNITY) THE SCHOOL LIBRARIAN EXHIBITS LIBRARY PROGRAM LEADERSHIP AND COLLABORATES WITHIN THE SCHOOL AND COMMUNITY TO PROMOTE THE SUCCESS OF ALL STUDENTS.**

Skill 4.1   **Advocates for the development of an exemplary library program that encourages excellence in all students.**

In *School Library Programs: Standards and Guidelines for Texas*, explicit guidelines outline what is required to be considered an exemplary library program.

Exemplary programs go well above and beyond the norm to meet the needs of their students. Factors that distinguish exemplary programs include:
- Maximum funding and support for media program.
- Strong focus on collaboration between media specialist and the school community.
- Has an outstanding collection of resources that exceeds state and national requirements.
- The program is student-centered.
- The program is constantly being evaluated to ensure students' needs are being met.
- Access to information is provided that lasts well beyond the school day and reaches beyond the school building.
- The media specialist forms partnerships within the community and beyond to provide resources for students.
- A wide array of professional development is offered to meet individual needs.
- Parents are strongly encouraged to participate in learning activities.

Skill 4.2   **Designs and uses statistical reports to support an exemplary library program.**

The school library media specialist continuously evaluates the program to ensure it meets the needs of the staff and students. Data is gathered through the Output and Evidence-Based Measures. This information is vital to the improvement of a media program. What is more effective is the presentation of this data to school and district administrators and the community.

Exemplary programs provide status reports to administrators on an annual basis. The report outlines the current situation, the direction in which the program should move and the necessary changes needed to ensure student growth.

Data gathered from evaluations can be helpful during the budgeting process. If weaknesses in the collection are noted then having hard data to show the deficiencies can support a request for additional funding.

By collecting data, the community can form a better understanding of the needs of the program especially when seeking to establish partnerships with outside agencies.

One of the key factors that evaluation data can show is media support for ensuring student mastery of state mandated curriculum.

Skill 4.3   Applies effective leadership strategies within campus and district administrative structures to promote library program goals.

A good leader should be able to work and inspire others to work in a team environment where the input of team members at all levels is encouraged and appreciated. To accomplish this goal, she should:

1.   Exhibit the desire to achieve the goals of an efficient library media program.
2.   Show appreciation for the contributions of library media staff and supervise them in a democratic style.
3.   Delegate tasks to responsible staff members.
4.   Engage in continuing education.
5.   Maintain active membership in professional organizations.
6.   Show respect and concern for colleagues and superiors.

One of the single most important parts of a successful leadership of a school library media program is collaboration between the school library media specialist and classroom teachers.

To support the collaborative process there are key skills the media specialist must possess. These include:
- Flexibility – have the ability to adjust to the differing needs of staff and students and flexibility with time
- Curriculum Expert – get to know the curriculum being taught at the grade levels being served. This makes the media specialist and invaluable partner.
- Leadership – set the path in which the media program should move towards, set goals and expectations, be the advocate for the teachers as well as the media program

- Approachable – establish good rapport with staff and students. Be someone they know will be willing to go above and beyond
- Persistence- to keep going and keep the media program moving forward

Skill 4.4 Promotes awareness of, respect for, and responsiveness to learning differences and diversity within the school and community.

Do not underestimate the power of the school library when striving to develop cultural awareness among students. The American Library Association strongly advocates the use of the school library media program to address and celebrate the diverse populations within a school. There are simple ways a media program can address this topic:

- Provide resources that address a variety of cultures. This should include both fiction and non-fiction works.
- Plan celebrations that focus upon various cultures or student populations.
- Invite guest speakers related to these topics.

Skill 4.5 Communicates effectively through oral, written, electronic, and nonverbal expression.

The school library media specialist must possess effective communication skills. They are the primary advocate for their program and must work diligently to promote it.

The media specialist must be able to clearly explain the mission and goals of the program to all members of the learning community. Through the sharing of current research regarding school library media centers and through the assessment of the program itself the school library media specialist identifies strengths and needs. Items used to effectively increase awareness for the program include fliers, presentations, letters, brochures and other forms of communication.

The ability to create and provide accurate reports and sharing them with teachers, administrators and parents is crucial. Ineffective communication in this arena could effect funding or program goals.

Skill 4.6 Establishes partnerships with businesses, learning institutions, global communities, organizations, and other libraries to strengthen programs and support campus goals.

The school library media program is no longer an isolated entity within a school. One of the most valuable things they can do to promote the library media program is to develop partnerships within the community. Research has shown that strong parental and community involvement can increase student achievement.

When considering the forming of partnerships the school library media specialist must first examine the curriculum for the grade levels it serves as well as the goals for the media program. This will help to determine the people, agencies, and organizations that will best help meet student needs.

To begin the process, the school library media specialist must contact the agency to see what possible programs they have available for students. He/she can also explain the particular curriculum needs to see if the agency is willing to provide any needed services or resources.

Reasons for partnerships may include
- the location of additional programs or resources to expand student learning experience.
- gaining financial support for library or school projects.
- locating sites off campus where the library may hold special programs to support curricular needs.
- the school library media specialist becoming more involved in community improvement in support of the school.
- developing a greater knowledge of concerns and issues within the community as a whole and their impact on the school.

Skill 4.7   Develops library programs that offer families opportunities to participate in school activities and in their children's education.

One of the most effective ways to promote literacy as well as the school library media program is to create activities that involve the entire family. There are a variety of avenues that could be taken when planning family activities.

Activities centered around reading and literacy are very popular. Plan a family reading night where families come to school early in the evening to participate in things like storytelling, book making, meeting guest authors, and other literacy centered activities.

Parent workshops are very effective in increasing parent involvement. Most parents want to do everything they can to enhance their child's learning. Plan workshops that teach reading strategies to parents. They can support their child when reading at home. Parenting topics are also valuable. With the influx of technology in recent decades, teaching parents the skills that their students need to know to be more effective learners.

The possibilities are endless and could include math celebrations, science celebration, and cultural activities.

Skill 4.8 **Develops and implements a comprehensive public relations program (e.g., news media, Web pages, newsletters) that effectively involves and informs multiple constituencies.**

Building support for the school library media program creates a network of individuals willing to work to enhance the learning experiences for students. It all begins with a program mission that supports advocacy.

Media specialists have access to many resources that can be used to promote their program. One essential tool is the creation of a media center web page or website. Many people rely on the Internet to get information and information regarding the media program is no different. The site could include study tips, reading lists, event information and any detail your patrons need to know about using the media center and information literacy.

Use your local news media to publicize upcoming events. Place stories in the local paper to highlight media center happenings. If your district has a program on a local television station, enlist students to create a commercial for the media center.

More traditional forms of promotion include newsletters that highlight resources and letters to parents.

The American Library Association has developed an Advocacy Toolkit to assist libraries in promoting their programs. Parts of this toolkit include;

- @ Your Library program – outlines the role of the school library media specialist and the programs they manage
- there are PowerPoint presentations that explain @ your library and provide topics of discussion
- implementation plan for Information Power
- brochures for promoting advocacy
- guides for meeting with government officials
- resource guides for promoting the media center, intellectual freedom and other topics
- communication handbook

DOMAIN III.	LIBRARIANSHIP,
	INFORMATION SCIENCE, AND TECHNOLOGY

COMPETENCY 5   (LIBRARIANSHIP AND INFORMATION SCIENCE) THE SCHOOL LIBRARIAN APPLIES KNOWLEDGE OF LIBRARIANSHIP AND INFORMATION SCIENCE TO HELP THE SCHOOL COMMUNITY LOCATE, EVALUATE, AND USE INFORMATION TO SOLVE PROBLEMS AND TO ENCOURAGE LIFELONG READING AND LEARNING.

Skill 5.1   Understands the role of all types of libraries and information agencies in an integrated learning environment.

National guidelines for school library media programs are provided in documents published by the American Association of School Librarians (AASL), a division of the American Library Association (ALA), and the Association for Educational Communications and Technology (AECT).

Information Power: Guidelines for School Library Media Programs a collaboration of AASL/AECT, was published in 1988 to provide standardized national guidelines as a vision for school library media programs into the 21st century. The AASL/AECT Standards Writing Committee and contributors from public school districts and universities across the country, using standards that have been revised over the last thirty years, created a definitive work.

These revised standards reflect the flexibility to manage today's library media centers and to direct centers into the future. The AASL/AECT mission objectives are echoed in President Bush's message during a speech at the 1991 White House Conference on Library and Information Services. The following is a summary of the guidelines culled from these and other publications.

1.   A democratic society guarantees the right of its populace to be well-informed. To this end, libraries and media centers of all kinds are the bastions of intellectual freedom.

2.   Literacy for all United States residents begins in the public school system. School readiness through access to ample media stimuli, facilities that provide physical access to materials across cultural and economic barriers, and a sound national goal, supported by legislative funding, will ensure that Americans can avail themselves of the information to which they are entitled.

3.   Americans will become more productive in the workplace by taking advantage of the technology offered in the Information Age. To support the school-to-work initiative, school library media centers must offer access and instruction in emerging technologies used in business and industry.

4.   Collaborative efforts between schools, business, and community agencies will encourage life-long learning. *Information Power's* mission statement and the vision statements of many public schools specify life-long learning as their primary objective. Thus libraries, even in the schools, must become community centers, offering their materials and services to all segments of the public. Such open access also motivates school-aged students as they see adults continually seeking information and educational opportunities.

Note: Specific guidelines addressing personnel, budgets, resources and equipment, facilities, and leadership are included in discussions of performance indicators throughout this guide.

Skill 5.2   Understands the role of the school library program as a central element in the intellectual life of the school.

School libraries have moved away from simply housing a collection of resources to serving as the central element of the school. The school library media program serves to provide students with the information they need to become lifelong learning.

Key factors that influence this role include:

- Adequate staffing levels to support the number of staff and students.
- A strong collaborative relationship between the media specialist and teaching staff.
- The development of a program that supports authentic learning experiences.
- Full administrative support.
- Effective integration of information literacy skills into the curriculum.
- Adequate funding to support program efforts.
- Appropriate short and long-range plans to support student learning and the school's mission and goals.
- Ongoing evaluation to ensure the program is effective at meeting the needs of the learning community.
- Management of financial, material and human resources.

Skill 5.3 **Applies knowledge of theories, principles, and skills related to collection development (e.g., evaluating, selecting, and acquiring resources).**

Each school library media center should develop a policy tailored to the philosophy and objectives of that school's educational program. This policy provides guidelines by which all participants in the selection process can get insight into their responsibilities. The policy statement should reflect the following factors.

1. Compatibility with district, state, regional, and national guidelines (1.2).
2. Adherence to the principles of intellectual freedom and the specifics of copyright law.
3. Recognition of the rights of individuals or groups to challenge policies, procedures, or selected items and the establishment of procedures for dealing fairly with such challenges.
4. Recognition of users needs and interests, including community demographics.

The policy should include the school library media center's mission and the criteria used in the selection process. General criteria for the selection of all media include

1. Authenticity. Media should be accurate, current, and authoritative. Copyright or printing dates are indicators of currency, but examination of content is often necessary to determine the relevance of the subject matter to its intended use. Research into the reputations of contributors and comparison to other materials by the same producer will provide insight into its literary quality.

2. Subject matter appropriateness. Suitability to the school's educational objectives, scope of coverage, treatment and arrangement of content, importance of content to the user, and appropriateness to users' ability levels and learning styles must be considered.

3. Appeal. Consideration of the artistic quality and language appropriateness will help in the selection of media that students will enjoy using. Properly selected materials should stimulate creativity and inspire further learning.

Elements of a collection development plan:
1. Knowledge of the existing collection or the ability to create a new collection.
2. Knowledge of the external environment (the school and community).
3. Assessment of school programs and user needs.
4. Development of overall policies and procedures.
5. Guidelines for specific selection decisions.
6. Evaluation criteria.

7.   Establishment of a process for planning and implementing the collection plan.
8.   Establishment of acquisition policies and procedures.
9.   Establishment of maintenance program.
10.   Establishment of procedures for evaluating the collection.

Procedures for implementing the plan

1.   Learn the collection. A library media specialist, new to a school with an existing collection, should use several approaches to becoming familiar with the collection.
      a.   Browse the shelves. Note your degree of familiarity with titles. Examine items that are unfamiliar to you. Determine the relationship between the materials on similar subjects in different formats. Include the reference and professional collections in your browse. Consider the accessibility of various media and the ease with which they can be located by users.
      b.   Locate the center's procedures manual. Determine explanations for any seeming irregularities in the collection.
      c.   Determine if any portions of the collection are housed in areas outside the media center.

If the library media specialist is required to create a new collection, she should
      a.   Consult with the district director about new school collection policies.
      b.   Examine the collections of other comparable schools.
      c.   Examine companies, like Baker and Taylor's, who establish new collections based on criteria provided by the school.

2.   Learn about the community.
      a.   Examine the relationship of the media center to the total school program and other information agencies.
      b.   Become familiar with the school, cultural, economic and political characteristics of the community and their influence on the schools.
3.   Study the school's curriculum and the needs of the users (students and faculty). Examine the proportions of basic skills to enrichment offerings, academic or vocational courses, and requirements and electives. Determine the ability levels and grouping techniques for learners. Determine instructional objectives of teachers in various content areas or grade levels (3.13).
4.   Examine existing policies and procedures for correlation to data acquired in researching the school and community.
5.   Examine specific selection procedures to determine if guidelines are best met.
6.   Examine evaluation criteria for effectiveness in maintaining an appropriate collection.

7.   Examine the process to determine that accurate procedures are in place to meet the criteria.
8.   Examine the acquisition plan. Determine the procedure by which materials are ordered, received, paid for and processed.
9.   Examine maintenance procedures for repairing or replacing materials and equipment, replacing consumables, and discarding non-repairable items.
10. Examine the policies and procedures for evaluation, then examine the collection itself to determine if policies and procedures are contributing to quality and quantity (4.6.5).

Procedures for maintaining the collection are perhaps the most important in the collection plan. The plan itself must provide efficient, economical procedures for keeping materials and equipment in usable condition.

Maintenance policies for equipment and some policies for materials are determined at the district level (4.6.3). Procedures to satisfy these policies are followed at the building level.

1.   Replacement or discard of damaged items based on comparison of repair to replacement cost. Districts usually maintain repair contracts with external contractors for major repairs that cannot be done at the school or district media service center.
2.   Equipment inventory and records on repair or disposal. Usage records help with the transfer of usable items from school to school.
3.   Book bindery contracts.

Policies and procedures for periodic inspection, preventive maintenance and cleaning, and minor repairs are established and conducted at the school media center.

1.   Print material. Spine and jacket repairs, taping torn pages and replacing processing features.
2.   Non-print materials. Cleaning, splicing, repairing cases.
3.   Equipment. Cleaning, bulb replacement.
4.   Inventory and weeding of print and non-print materials; regular replacement of worn or outdated equipment.
5.   Record-keeping on items that have been lost or stolen, damaged by nature or neglect, or transferred/discarded.
6.   Security systems operation, procedures for emergency disasters, and safe storage of duplicate records.

District collection development policies may be general or specific but always address areas of concern to all schools. The policy statement should reflect the philosophy of the district, indicate the legal responsibility of the school board, and the delegation of authority to specific individuals at the district and school level.

One statement will usually address all instructional materials, including textbook and library media resources.

Some objectives which might be included in the policy:

1. To provide resources that contain information that supports and enhances the school's curriculum.
2. To provide resources that satisfy user needs, abilities, and learning styles.
3. To provide resources that develop literary appreciation and artistic values.
4. To provide resources that reflect the culture and ethnic diversity of society and the contributions of members of various groups to our country's heritage.
5. To provide materials that enable students to solve problems and make judgments relevant to real life.
6. To provide resources that present opposing views on historical or contemporary issues so that students may learn to think critically and objectively.

District plans may deal with

1. Funding policies.
    a. Allocation. School media centers generally receive a portion of the general operating budget. The total amount is determined by a per student dollar amount and may come directly from the district media accounts or, under school-based management, may be apportioned from school budget categories.
    b. Authorization for purchases. These policies vary depending on who has control of the budget: principal, district or media supervisor, district purchasing agent or any combination of the three. In some districts purchase requests must also be approved by curriculum supervisors.
    c. Supplemental sources. Federal or state block grants, endowments, or district capital outlay funds are allocated on a per capita or special project allotment basis. Responsibility for preparation of grant applications is supervised or conducted at the district level. Some districts also set policy concerning the suitability of private donations of material or property items.
2. Preview of considered materials. Some districts seek total control of previewing.
3. Collection size. Districts will frequently set minimum materials and equipment levels, especially if they aim to meet SAC accreditation standards. SAC standard 5.4.1 specifies a minimum book collection which is approximately 10 volumes per student. Responsibility for start-up collections at new schools are governed by district media.
4. Resource sharing. Some decisions in regards to delivery systems, cooperative funding, software licensing and liability are district determined.

5. Time constraints. All districts require that funds be expended by a specific deadline.

6. District media library policies and procedures. Materials that are either too expensive for school budgets and will be used by more than one school are maintained at the district library.

7. Equipment and materials maintenance and repair policy. Districts maintain repair contracts and set procedures for their use. Annual inventories, especially of equipment, are required and periodic assessment of policies are conducted.

8. Central processing. Available in some districts, this department processes materials for convenience and uniformity.

From time to time libraries will receive challenges regarding the content of library resources. It is important for schools to have a reconsideration policy for challenged books. According the American Library Association's(ALA) *Library Bill of Rights*, libraries are sources of information that should cover all points of view on all topics following the rules of The First Amendment. The association does not believe that information should be removed from the library for any reason if it fit the criteria of the selection policy.

Many school districts have a reconsideration policy in place. If a district does not, a good place to go for assistance is the ALA website. Here are a few things to consider.

1. Develop a principles statement for your library that expresses the school's position regarding access to information. *The Library Bill of Rights* will be a good reference for wording such a statement.

2. Outline a procedure for handling the challenged material. This could include notifying the principal when a challenge arises, procedures to follow if the complaint cannot be resolved informally, developing forms to file for formal complaints, library advisory committee responsibilities, and how to notify the person filing the complaint of the reconsideration committee's decision.

3. It is important to lay out the responsibilities of the school level reconsideration committee so that they will understand the procedures for handling the complaint.

It is important to make sure the resources in the school library's collection is current and meets the needs of the students. One way to accomplish this is by mapping the collection.

Collection mapping is the practice of examining the quantity and quality of your resource collection. A collection map will provide a graphic display of the extent of the collection. In other words, the collection map offers a quick snapshot of the collection.

The resource collection should be divided into three areas:

1. There should be a base or core collection that provides something for everyone.
2. There should be general emphasis collections that cover curricular needs for specific subjects and/ or grade levels.
3. There should be specific emphasis collections that are used to cover the needs of particular units or topics.

Collection maps have many benefits. These include:

- identifying strengths and weaknesses within the collection
- do the resources match curriculum taught or state standards
- planning for purchases
- identifying sections in need of weeding
- demonstrating areas of need and areas of excellence

School libraries are sources of information for staff and students, therefore it is important that the information is current and of relevance. While most schools have a selection policy it is also important to have a weeding policy. Weeding the collection requires the school library media specialist to remove outdated information or worn books from the shelves.

There are many resources that provide assistance with weeding procedures. A few things to take into consideration when reviewing your collection for weeding are:

3. Weeding should be an ongoing process.
4. Review books for age, frequency of use, condition, multiple copies, and accuracy of information
5. Here are the suggested weeding procedures for each Dewey level:
    - 000 – encyclopedias every five years, other materials no more than eight years
    - 100 – five to eight years
    - 200 – can be high turnover with religious books – keep current
    - 300 – almanacs replace every two years, keep political information current
    - 400 – check for wear and tear frequently
    - 500 -- continuously update to make sure scientific information is current
    - 600 -- continuously update medical information as older information can be misleading or dangerous
    - 700 – keep until worn
    - 800 – keep until worn
    - 900 – weed about every two years
    - Biography – keep most current or best written titles
    - Adult fiction – weed for multiple copies, keep those in best shape and that have the most literary value
    - Young-adult and children's fiction – same as adult fiction
    - Reference – weed for currency and accuracy

Skill 5.4   Applies standard procedures (e.g., AACR, Dewey, LCSH, MARC) for classifying, cataloging, and processing resources.

Two classification systems are prevalent in the United States.

1.   The Library of Congress System Heading uses a system which has been adopted by many colleges and universities since the 1960's. This is usually comprised of five large red volumes that are housed in the reference section.
2.   The Dewey Decimal System is used predominately in schools and public libraries.
 The purpose of both systems is to provide universal standards of organizing collections. These systems facilitate location of materials within a collection and enable institutions to share information and materials that are uniformly grouped.

The MARC format is relatively universal and enables a school library to utilize many commercial automation tools. The format allows for unlimited fields which provide more efficient cataloging for both print and non-print items. Each field is marked with a tag. A tag represents a specific piece of information i.e. 245 tag lists title information and the 520 tag marks the summary.

The MARC format assists in preserving bibliographic integrity. Bibliographic integrity refers to the accuracy and uniformity with which items are catalogued.

Skill 5.5   Applies knowledge of theories, principles, and skills related to organization, storage, and retrieval of resources.

Following a standard set of international rules, *Anglo-American Cataloguing Rules(AACR2)*, enables users to locate materials equally well in all libraries that subscribe to these rules. To maintain this integrity, catalogers

1.   Recognize an International Standard Bibliographic Description (ISBD) that establishes the order in which bibliographic elements will appear in catalog entries.
2.   Note changes that occur after each five years review of ISBD.
3.   Agree to catalog all materials using the AACR standards.

The components of a basic bibliographic record (may be used in Library of Congress Classification (LCC) or Dewey Decimal Classification (DDC) shelflist cards or in Online Computer Library Center's (OCLC) MARC records for automated systems):

1.   Call Number. Includes DDC or LCCN classification number followed by a book identification identifier (numerals or letters).
2.   Author Main Entry Heading. Use name by which author is most commonly known even if that name is a pseudonym.

3.	Title and Statement of Responsibility Area. Include title, subtitle, or parallel titles and name(s) of authors, editors, illustrators, translators, or groups functioning in authorship capacity.

4.	Edition Statement. Provide ordinal number of edition.

5.	Material Specific Details. Used with only four materials (computer files, cartographic materials, printed music, and serials in all formats).

6.	Publication, Distribution, etc. Area. Include place of publication, name of publisher and copyright date.

7.	Physical Description Area. Include the extent of the work (number of pages, volumes, or other units); illustrative matter; size/dimensions; and accompanying materials.

8.	Series. Provide title of series and publication information if different from statement of responsibility.

9.	Notes. Provide information to clarify any other descriptive components, including audio-visual formats or reading levels.

10.	Standard numbers. Provide ISBN, ISSN, or LCC number, price, or other terms of availability.

There are three levels of bibliographic description.

1.	Level 1 descriptions are the simplest and most appropriate for small or general collections. Although they satisfy AACR standards, they are not considered full records.

2.	Level 2 descriptions are more detailed and are used by medium to large libraries where clients use materials for research. Many libraries, including small media centers, use description format somewhere between Level 1 and Level 2.

3.	Level 3 descriptions are full records that require application of every AACR rule. Most major libraries, even the Library of Congress, develop some system just short of full Level 3 cataloging.

OCLC bibliographic records (MARC) use both a short form (Level I enhanced) and a long form (Level 2).

It is necessary for all entries to have standardized subject headings. *Sear's List of Subject Headings* is generally used in Dewey Decimal classification while the Library of Congress has its own subject heading list.

### Skill 5.6	Applies bibliographic and retrieval techniques for organizing and using information sources.

When searching for information the researcher first begins with the topic. Write down words or phrases that directly related to the topic being covered. Start with general terms and then break it down into more specific areas. These terms become the keywords that will be used in the search. A keyword is an important word or phrase that is used to retrieve information.

Once the keyword(s) has been determined, use it to search books, articles, or electronic resources. When searching through print materials the researcher will look for specific subject headings. Subject headings are words or phrases that are used to locate resources by topics.

When information can be found under more than one subject heading the information is often cross-referenced. The words "See also" may be used to direct the researcher to a more appropriate heading.

When using print references is can be helpful to consult an index to locate the keyword or any cross-referenced topics.

Electronic resources offer a wider array of strategies for locating information. Two of the most common strategies can be explained as follows:

- Boolean operators: Popular operators include:
  - AND – ex. Lions and tigers – both words must be found in the searched text
  - AND NOT – ex. Lions AND NOT tigers – lions must be listed, but do not return listings that contain the word tigers
  - OR – ex. Lions OR tigers – may contain either word

- Wildcards: This is an effective tool if one is unsure of the spelling or date for the topic being searched. An example would include the search for a list of all names in a database beginning with the letters ph. One way to phrase the search is to type PH* . The asterisk at the end will cause the search to return anything in the database that begins with the letters "PH".

Skill 5.7 Effectively interviews patrons to determine information needs.

To determine the information needs of a patron it may be necessary to conduct a reference interview. The reference interview is a dialog between the media specialist and the patron. It should be conducted in a relaxed manner and not feel like an interrogation.

The interview should begin with open-ended questions. Open-ended questions are those questions that cannot be answered with just a yes or no. They require a person to be more specific. This type of questioning often begins with general questions that grow more specific as the media specialist uncovers the patron's needs. Types of open-ended interview questions would include:
- What type of information are you searching for?
- What is your topic?
- How much information do you need?
- What information do you have already?
- How will you use this information?
- When do you need to have the information

To further assist patrons the media specialist will need to ask some closed-end questions as well. Closed-end questions can be answered with a yes or no. Types of relevant closed-end questions include:

- Have you searched the card catalog?
- Do you need world wide web sites as well?
- Is this for a class assignment?

It may be more difficult to determine the needs of some patrons. There are variables that can affect the progress of an interview.
- Patron familiarity with resources and how to locate them.
- Age of patron.
- Patron's knowledge of the type of information they need.
- How comfortable the patron feels in asking for assistance.

The most important thing to remember is that the media specialist is there to provide a service to the staff and students. They should treat all patrons with the utmost courtesy.

Skill 5.8   Applies knowledge of literature and information resources to help patrons select materials.

There are a wide variety of resources available online to assist school library media specialists with providing access to current information. Below are listed several information resources.

Periodical Directories

Ulrich's International Periodicals Directory
- complete and current reference for select periodicals and serials
- information collected from over 80,000 worldwide serials publishers
- contains annuals, continuations, conference proceedings

SIRS Enduring Issues
- print versions contains eight volumes and 32-topics
- highlights the best articles published during the preceding year

Public Affairs Information Service (PAIS)
- references over 553,300 journal articles, books, documents directories and reports
- offered online

Indexes

The New York Times
- assists with locating articles and information printed in the New York Times newspaper.
- Searchable by topic and uses the words "see also" to suggest other subject headings

Professional Journals

The Library Quarterly
- scholarly research regarding all areas of librarianship

School Library Media Research
- published by American Association of School Librarians
- the successor to *School Library Media Quarterly Online*
- purpose is to provide research concerning the management, implementation, and evaluation of school library media programs.

Library Trends
- explores critical trends in professional librarianship
- includes practical applications and literature reviews

Library Power
- research study that proved the viability of school libraries as a vehicle to promote student achievement

American Libraries
- published by the American Library Association
- provides the latest news and updates from the association

School Library Journal
- serves school and public librarians who work with young
- provides information needed to integrate libraries into all aspects of the school curriculum
- provides resources to become effective technology leaders
- provides resources to assist with collection development

VOYA (Voice of Youth Advocates)
- focuses on librarians and educators working with young adults
- founded by Dorothy M. Broderick and Mary K. Chelton

School Library Media Activities Monthly Magazine
- designed for K-8 school library media specialists
- focuses on collaboratively planned units with teachers
- stresses importance of introducing reference materials

Knowledge Quest
- published by The American Association of School Librarians
- designed to assist with the development of school library media programs

Skill 5.9   Employs a variety of techniques (e.g., reading materials, media, programs, motivational strategies) to guide the development of independent readers.

Motivating students to read helps to develop a love of reading and the development of independent readers. One factor in motivating students to read is to have a media collection that covers a wide range of topics in various formats.

Special programs such as the Texas Reading Club encourage students to read during the summer months. Students who complete the program are recognized.

Having students participate by voting to select the Texas Bluebonnet Award winner provides them with a sense of ownership and motivates them to read. Students can vote only if they have read at least five books on the list.

Finally, reading lists are an important tool in guiding parents, teachers and students to appropriate level books as noted in the Bluebonnet, Tayshas, Lone Star, and 2 X 2 Reading Lists.

Skill 5.10   Understands and applies principles of ethical behavior (e.g., intellectual freedom, information access, privacy, intellectual property) in various professional contexts.

The principles of intellectual freedom are guaranteed by the First Amendment to the Constitution of the United States. They are reinforced in the Library Bill of Rights adapted by the ALA in 1948, the AECT's statement on intellectual freedom (1978), the freedom to read and review statements of the ALA (1953 and 1979), and the National Council of English Teachers, Students Right to Read Statement.

The principles as they relate to children:

1.   Freedom of access to information in all formats through activities that develop critical thinking and problem solving skills.
2.   Freedom of access to ideas that present a variety of points of view through activities that teach discriminating reading.
3.   Freedom to acquire information reflective of the intellectual, physical, and social growth of the user.

It becomes the responsibility of the school library media specialist to develop and maintain a collection development policy that ensures these freedoms.

Copyright Infringement
When a suspected infringement of copyright is brought to the attention of the school library media specialist, she should follow certain procedures.

1.   Determine if a violation has in effect occurred. Never accuse or report alleged instances to a higher authority without verification.
2.   If an instance is verified, tactfully inform the violator of the specific criteria to use so that future violations can be avoided. Presented properly, the information will be accepted as constructive.
3.   If advise is unheeded and further infractions occur, bring them to the attention of the teacher's supervisor - a team leader or department chair - who can handle the matter as an evaluation procedure.
4.   Inform the person who has reported the alleged violation of the procedures being used.

Intellectual Freedom Issue
Despite the best collection development policies, an occasional complaint will arise. In our society the following issues cause controversy: politics, gay rights, profanity, pornography, creationism vs. evolution, the occult, sex education, racism and violence. Adults disagree philosophically about these issues. They will often express their concern first to the school library media specialist. Ethically, he is bound to protect the principles of intellectual freedom, but he is also bound by those same principles to treat the complaint seriously as the expression of an opposing view.

The most important thing is not to panic. The challenge is not an affront to the media specialist but a complaint about the content, language, or graphics in a material. The first step is to greet the complainant calmly and explain the principles of intellectual freedom you are bound to uphold. A good paraphrase from the AECT Statement is that a learner's right to access information can only be abridged by an agreement between parent and child. With the current emphasis on the V chip for selective television viewing, are becoming more aware of their own roles in censoring unwanted images from their children. In most instances, a calm, rational discussion will satisfy the challenger.

However, if the challenge is pursued, the media specialist will have to follow district procedures for handling the complaint. The appropriate school administrator should be informed. Of course, an administrator may have been confronted initially. In either instance the complainant is asked to fill out a formal complaint form, citing his specific objection in a logical manner. Sometimes, simply thinking the issue through clearly and recognizing that someone will truly listen to his complaint is enough of a solution. If all else fails, a reconsideration committee should be appointed to take the matter under advisement and recommend a course of action.

Confidentiality Issue

Suggested procedures include the following[1]:

1. When a request is made, explain the confidentiality policy
2. Consult with the appropriate legal to determine if such process, order, or subpoena is in good form and if there is a just cause for its issuance.
3. If the process is not in proper form or if just cause has not been shown, the library should insist that this be remedied before any records are released.
4. Generally a subpoena *duces tecum* (bring your records) requires the responsible library officer to attend court or to provide testimony at his or her deposition. It also may require that certain circulation records be submitted.
5. Staff should be trained and required to report any threats not supported by a process, order, or subpoena concerning the records.
6. If any problems arise refer them to the responsible legal council.

Skill 5.11   Demonstrates a commitment to the library profession (e.g., membership in professional organizations, participation in continuing education, collaboration with other information professionals).

Professional development allows the school library media specialist to stay abreast of current trends in school library media programs.

- The media specialist should be actively involved in national, state, and local Library Media Organizations such as:
  National:
  American Library Association (ALA)
  American Association of School Library (AASL)
  International Reading Association (IRA)
  Association for Supervision and Curriculum Development (ASCD)
  National Staff Development Council (NSCD)
  State
  Texas Computer Education Association (TCEA)
  Texas Library Association (TLA)
  Texas Association of School Librarians (TASL)
- The media specialist should attend national, state, and regional conferences annually such as:
  Technology Education Conferences
  National Educational Computing Conference
- The media specialist should subscribe to at least three library or education-related publications.
- The media specialist should participate in discussion forums such as LM_NET

COMPETENCY 6   **(INFORMATION ACCESS AND TECHNOLOGY)
THE SCHOOL LIBRARIAN USES AND INTEGRATES
TECHNOLOGY, TELECOMMUNICATIONS, AND
INFORMATION SYSTEMS TO ENRICH THE
CURRICULUM, ENHANCE LEARNING, AND PROMOTE
THE SUCCESS OF THE SCHOOL COMMUNITY.**

Skill 6.1   **Understands basic terms and concepts of current technology
(e.g., hardware, software applications and functions,
input/output devices, networks).**

Hardware – The physical parts of the computer such as the central processing
unit (CPU), monitor, keyboard, etc.

Software- Computer programs that tell a computer what to do; instructions to the
CPU to tell it what to do with the data it receives.

Input devices- The parts or a computer which are used to add data into a
computer. (Ex: keyboard, mouse, scanner, touch screen, probeware device)

Output devices- Parts used to display data from a computer. (Ex: printer, monitor,
speaker)

Functions- calculations that reuse frequently repeated complex worksheet
formulas.

Network- A system of computers linked together to share data, software, and
hardware

Wide Area Network (WAN)- A computer network that spans a relatively large
geographical area. Typically, a Wide Area Network consists of two or more local-
area networks

Local Area Network (LAN)- A group of computers, connected by cables, set up in
a single location such as a school or office which allows the sharing of resources.

File Extensions - One or several letters at the end of a filename. These usually
follow a period after a filename (.dot) and indicate the type of information stored
in the file. Examples:
- .jpg or .jpeg – (joint photographic experts group) picture file
- .gif – (graphics interchange format) picture file
- .bmp – (bitmap) picture file
- .png – (portable network graphics) picture file
- .doc – document file
- .txt – text file
- .pdf – (portable document format)
- .html – (hypertext markup language) web page file

Skill 6.2   Evaluates, acquires, analyzes, and manages digital resources (e.g., databases, network information) and assesses information for accuracy and validity.

As students begin to search for information resources for research or other projects it is important to evaluate the resources selected for their effectiveness.

There are several key factors to consider when looking at any type of resource be it book or web page.

These criteria include:

1. Audience: Who was this information intended to reach? What is the level of the information?

2. Scope: How detailed is the information? Is this work focused on an overall outline of the topic or does it provide in depth information on one specific aspect of the topic?

3. When was the information published? How often is the website updated?

4. Who is the author? What authority does this person have to be writing this article?

5. Is the article free from bias? Is it from a single person or an organization trying to argue for a certain position?

6. Does the author include their resource bibliography?

7. Does the information come from a scholarly article/ magazine or from a popular article/ magazine?

Skill 6.3   Uses existing and emerging technologies to access, evaluate, and disseminate information for library and instructional programs.

Technology provides an avenue for communication that is increasingly expanding. Traditional methods such as email and discussion forums are giving way to videoconferencing and live audio discussions. The technology available makes it easier than ever to share information well beyond the traditional school day.

Tools such as online catalogs allow patrons to search for resources from home and place requests to check out the materials when they return to school.

One of the most widely adopted uses of technology in education is in providing distance learning opportunities. The school library media center can play an essential role in providing distance learning opportunities.

Distance learning takes place in any situation where the student and the instructor are in separate locations. The learning can take place in real time and be interactive or can be pre-recorded and viewed at a different time. The teaching may take place in an online venue such as the widely used Blackboard where must of the class discussion occurs during chat sessions or via discussion board.

Benefits of distance learning include:
- Flexibility – students can access and respond to information outside of a normal schedule
- Increased opportunity – distance learning may provide learning experiences for students that may not be possible in their current location
- Multi-sensory experience – distance learning opportunities may include video, digital images, audio, etc. thus reaching a variety of learning styles.
- Affordability – it may be more cost effective to take advantage of a distance learning class than to hire a teacher to teach only a few students
- Instruction for homebound students

School library media coordinators can take advantage of distance learning activities to increase student access to resources. Not only are distance learning classes offered by colleges, universities, and other secondary education entities, but programs provided by museums, science organizations and other public venues as well. When the school library media specialist collaborates with these units they can increase student access not only to information but to the specialists who provide such information.

When considering distance learning opportunities it is crucial to consider the technology needed to make it a success. One mode of instructional delivery is through video conferencing. When working with large groups an information highway room that is equipped with multiple video cameras, microphones and a large screen video display may be used. For smaller groups or one-on-one delivery a web camera used in conjunction with special software may be just as effective as a larger system. With all of these tools it is necessary to make sure that the computing equipment meets minimum requirements and that there is enough bandwidth to support a large volume of data being sent along the network. Bandwidth would be the speed in which data can be transferred.

Through all of this the school library media coordinator oversees both the technical and instructional pieces to ensure patrons have every advantage possible.

Skill 6.4   Uses interlibrary loan to facilitate information access beyond the campus.

Resource sharing has always been an integral part of education. Before the technology revolution, the sharing was done within schools or departments and between teachers. Now it is possible to access information around the world.

One of the most prevalent forms of resource sharing in school libraries is the use of interlibrary loans. This can mean the sharing of media resources between school in the district or forming partnerships with the local public library. Either format provides benefits for all involved. Examples include:

1.   Providing a broader information base to enable users to find and access the resources that provide the needed information.
2.   Reducing or containing media center budgets.
3.   Establishing cooperation with other resource providers that encourage mutual planning and standardization of control.

Skill 6.5   Uses productivity tools to communicate information in various formats (e.g., newsletters, multimedia presentations, Web applications, teleconferencing).

There are many technology tools available that are meant to save time and increase productivity. The types of applications available will be determined by district adopted software. Apple Productivity Tools, Microsoft Office, and Lotus are groups of productivity tools that may include word processing, spreadsheets, databases and multimedia applications. Examples of types of productivity tools and their uses include:

- Word processing software- most effective for creating letters, reports, simple brochures, and flyers.
- Desktop publishing software – similar to word processing, but is designed to accommodate more complicated layouts for newsletters, brochures, cards, and certificates.
- Electronic calendars – Generally allow the users to share calendars with others, post and view appointments online, and can be viewed anywhere.
- Spreadsheets – Effectively managing media budgets is crucial. Spreadsheets can be used to track purchases and balances from multiple funding sources.
- Databases- Effective for organizing, managing, and retrieving resources. Databases can be used for collection management and managing inventory.
- Presentation Software- It is important for the media specialist to promote the media program. Multimedia presentations are effective tools for sharing information with others.

- Web Applications – Web pages can be created using simple html editors, WYSIWYG (What you see is what you get) software, or more complicated programs that create animations and interactive sites.
- Teleconferencing software- Allows the users to communicate over the Internet using audio and/or video.

Skill 6.6   Uses information problem-solving processes, activities, and materials to integrate the state-mandated curriculum for technology applications into the library program.

Texas Essential Knowledge and Skills (TEKS) stress the importance of integrating information and technology skills to assist with problem-solving processes. There are three main areas where technology works with this process and examples of how it can be used listed below.

1. Use appropriate technology to modify the solution to problems.
   Students can use audio, video, graphics or software to expand learning experiences through things like literature extension activities, creating presentations based upon information learned.

2. Use technology to communicate with others and enhance research skills.
   -Video conferencing and other online communication tools allow students to collaborate on projects with people in other parts of the world.
   -Simulations and virtual field trips allow students to visit places that may not be possible otherwise. This provides the student with the experience of actually being at the location themselves. Well-constructed simulations allow students to interact with the environment.

3. Use technology to evaluate both the process and product of information learned.
   -Tools such as spreadsheets allow students to gather, organize and display numerical data.
   - Presentation software allows students to share and present information to others.
   -Online tools provide students with a means to evaluate products.

Skill 6.7   Models successful search strategies using technology.

Whether searching for information in print indices or electronic resources, it is necessary to formulate strategies for locating information prior to beginning a search to save time and effort.

One of the first things that must be determined is the specific topic that is being researched. Narrow this down to the most specific term possible. This term will be the keyword for the search regardless if the source be print or electronic.

Electronic resources offer a wider array of strategies for locating information. Three of the most common strategies can be explained as follows:

- Boolean operators: Popular operators include:
  - AND – ex. Lions and tigers – both words must be found in the searched text
  - AND NOT – ex. Lions AND NOT tigers – lions must be listed, but do not return listings that contain the word tigers
  - OR – ex. Lions OR tigers – may contain either word

- Wildcards: This is an effective tool if one is unsure of the spelling or date for the topic being searched. An example would include the search for a list of all names in a database beginning with the letters ph. One way to phrase the search is to type PH* . The asterisk at the end will cause the search to return anything in the database that begins with the letters "PH".

- Quotations: The use of quotation marks is very helpful when searching for a specific phrase such as "Lone Star State". By placing quotes around the topic, the computer understands that all of these words must be listed in this exact format in all records retrieved. This greatly narrows search results. If the phrase was not listed using quotation marks the search would retrieve records that had any of the three words in their listing.

Skill 6.8   Guides students and staff to utilize established criteria (e.g., design, content delivery, audience, relevance) in the development of technology-based products.

In the last twenty years, audio-visual materials, once considered supplementary to instruction, have become instructional media, integral parts of the instructional process. Students and teachers should learn not only to use commercial products but to design and produce their own materials. It is appropriate for faculty to produce their own resources when:

1.   Commercial products are unavailable, unsuited to learning styles/preferences/environments, or too costly.
2.   Teaching styles indicate a preference for non-commercial products.
3.   Teachers have the expertise and necessary equipment for original production.

It is appropriate for students to produce their own resources when

1.   Achieving understanding with non-verbal means of expression.
2.   Communicating ideas and information to others.
3.   Expressing creativity.
4.   Demonstrating mastery of lesson objectives by alternative means.

Having determined that it is appropriate to use teacher or student/produced media, it is necessary to determine which media should be produced to meet the specific instructional need. School library media specialists may produce media for two purposes:

1. To make presentations for information skills instruction, other teacher-directed activities, or testing.
2. To make materials to be placed directly in the hands of students.

Many excellent books on media instruction detail the instructional uses of media formats. A few will be summarized here.

1. Introduction. Formats that allow large group listening or viewing are appropriate for introducing new materials: computer projection, overhead transparencies, and video. With young learners display boards with large print and audiocassettes for story- telling with non-readers are most effective.
2. Application. During this phase, media that lend themselves to individual or small group use are needed. As students Investigate the subject matter, organize that information, practice, or demonstrate understanding, they may create any or several types of media. With young children these would include manipulatives - building blocks, letters or numbers, or shapes - in cloth, plastic, or wood. Older students would create photographs/slides, audio, or video. Some secondary students might even design their own computer programs. Students at all levels can be taught to use computer design software to create multi-media productions.

The application of media production techniques helps the producer - adult or child - clarify his own objectives and determine the exact format which would best present his ideas and achieve his goals. A lesson on distinguishing the calls of local birds might use audio while recognizing plumage would use slides or videotape. Students preparing a study of estuarine ecology might incorporate video and computer graphics designed from electron microscope imagery to demonstrate types of micro-organisms in the local river.

Once the determination to produce media has been made, there is a process for planning, designing, and evaluating the product.

Planning:

1. State the main idea (goal) of the production, clearly and concisely.
2. Determine the purpose of the product.
   a. To provide information or develop appreciation. Media with this purpose is general in nature, usually meant for presentation to a class or larger group, and involves the audience as passive listeners. However, it must use dramatic or motivational appeals to hold audience interest.
   b. To provide instruction. Designed for individual or small group use, instructive media should be specific, systematic, and interactive.
3. Develop the objectives. State specifically what the audience should know or be able to do after using this media and what measurements will be used to determine their knowledge or ability.
4. Analyze the audience. Determine ability and interest, learning styles, and current understanding of the topic.
5. Research the idea. Use print, non-print, and human resources to study both the subject matter and the media techniques/formats to best present the subject matter.

Designing:

1. Prepare an outline of the content. Create story board cards for each subheading and match them to the objectives.
2. Select the media format(s) to communicate your idea. Consider time, effort, and cost as well as audio-visual needs. If motion or sound are not essential, consider using transparencies or slides which are easier to make and require no editing. Consider the equipment and facilities available.
3. Create the content. Prepare a story board delineating the description of each graphic and write a corresponding script if captions or sound narration will be included.
4. Create the media (3.4.4).

Evaluating:

1. Observe reaction of audience to resources. Body language and verbal reactions, especially in younger children, will indicate the level of interest.
2. Solicit verbal or written reactions to appearance, arrangement, and technical quality as well as ease of understanding and mastery of content.
3. Examine costs. Determine if costs of materials and time invested were equal to outcomes.

Skill 6.9   Participates in district, state, and national technology initiatives.

The school library media specialist is responsible for helping to prepare students to be 21st century citizen. An important part of this process is to stay abreast of the technology initiatives at various levels.

The media specialist needs to be actively involved in planning efforts at the school, district, and state levels. This allows the media specialist to shape the direction of current and future technology initiatives.

It is important for media specialists to stay abreast of state and national initiatives by subscribing to newsletters, participating in library related discussion boards, subscribing to journals and actively participate in national and state library associations.

One of the more recent national technology initiatives fell under the No Child Left Behind Act. States and school districts are required to create and implement both short and long range technology plans. The Texas Education Agency's Instructional Materials and Educational Technology Division works to manage the process at the state level.

Skill 6.10   Selects and utilizes automation systems, including OPAC on the Web, to provide maximum access to resources.

Automated circulation systems provide an easy and effective way to manage media resources. When considering the purchase of a system it is necessary to check district and state recommendations and requirements.

Circulation systems that provide web access to resources through Online Public Access Catalogs (OPAC) are most desirable. This allows patrons to access resources or lists of resources from any location at any time.

Schools can merge their online resource database to create a district union catalog which is perfect for initiating interlibrary loans. Merging resources maximizes the use of funds and expands the number of resources available for students. District union catalogs can merge to form a statewide union catalog.

Sample Test

DIRECTIONS: Read each item and select the best response.

1. **A good leader should:**
   (Skill 1.1) Easy

   A. delegate responsibility

   B. show respect for colleagues

   C. engage in continuing education

   D. all of the above

2. **The English I (9th Grade) teacher wants his students to become familiar with the contents of books in the reference area of the school library media center. He asks the library media specialist to recommend an activity to accomplish this goal. Which of the following activities would best achieve the goal?**
   (Skill 1.2) Average Rigor

   A. Assign a research paper on a specific social issues topic.

   B. Require a biography of a famous person.

   C. Design a set of questions covering a variety of topics and initiate a scavenger hunt approach to their location.

   D. Teach students the Dewey Decimal system and have them list several books in each Dewey subcategory.

3. The TAXONOMIES OF THE SCHOOL LIBRARY MEDIA PROGRAM outlines eleven levels of school library media specialists' involvement with curriculum and instruction and was developed by:
    (Skill 1.3) Rigorous

    A. Eisenberg.

    B. Bloom

    C. Loertscher

    D. Lance.

4. The school library media center should be an inviting space that encourages learning. To accomplish this the school library media specialist should do all of the following except:
    (Skill 1.3) Average rigor

    A. collaborate with school staff and students.

    B. create a schedule where each class comes to the media center each week for instruction.

    C. arrange materials so that they are easy to locate.

    D. promote the program as a wonderful place for learning.

5. To foster the collaborative process the media specialist must possess all of the following skills except:
    (Skill 1.3) Easy

    A. leadership

    B. flexibility

    C. perverse

    D. persistence

6. A cooperative relationship between a media specialist and a teacher is known as:
    (Skill 1.3) Average rigor

    A. collection development

    B. collaboration

    C. telecommunications

    D. flexible scheduling

7. **The media specialist is interested in beginning collaborative planning sessions with the teachers within the school, but not all of the teachers are interested. The media specialist should:**
(Skill 1.3) Average rigor

A.   wait until all of the teachers are interested

B.   have the principal make all teacher collaboratively plan with the media specialist

C.   work with the teachers who are most willing to engage in the process

D.   abandon the idea

8. **Steps in the Big6 Model include all of the following except:**
(Skill 1.4) Rigorous

A.   information seeking strategies

B.   location and access

C.   creation of information

D.   task definition

9. **Another popular information literacy model is:**
(Skill 1.4) Rigorous

A.   Bloom's Taxonomies

B.   Star Reader

C.   Pathways to Knowledge

D.   Follett Taxonomies

10. **The creators of the Big 6 Model are:**
(Skill 1.4) Average Rigor

A.   Eisenberg and Berkowitz.

B.   Marzano and Bloom.

C.   Bloom and Gardner.

D.   Lance and Eisenberg.

11. A secondary school social studies teacher reads an article in the current month's *Smithsonian* that clarifies points in the unit of study on the day prior to the scheduled unit test. He asks the media specialist if copyright law would allow copying the entire 3100 word article for distribution to each student in his two honors American history classes. The media specialist's proper response is that
(Skill 1.5) Rigorous

A. he can make only one copy and read it to the class.

B. he may not copy it because of the word length.

C. he may excerpt sections of it to meet the brevity test.

D. he may copy the needed multiples, allowed by the spontaneity test.

12. Section 108 of the Copyright Act permits the copying of an entire book if three conditions are met. Which of the following is NOT one of those conditions?
(Skill 1.5) Rigorous

A. The library intends to allow inter- library loan of the book.

B. The library is an archival library.

C. The copyright notice appears on all the copies.

D. The library is a public library.

13. Under the copyright brevity test, an educator may reproduce without written permission
(Skill 1.5) Rigorous

A. 10% of any prose or poetry work.

B. 500 words from a 5000 word article.

C. 240 words of a 2400 word story.

D. no work over 2500 words.

14. **Licensing has become a popular means of copyright protection in the area of**
(Skill 1.5) Average Rigor

A. duplicating books for interlibrary loan.

B. use of software application on multiple machines.

C. music copying.

D. making transparency copies of books or workbooks that are too expensive to purchase.

15. **"Fair Use" policy in videotaping off-air from commercial television requires**
(Skill 1.5) Rigorous

A. show in 5 days, erase by the 20th day.

B. show in 10 days, erase by the 30th day.

C. show in 10 days, erase by the 45th day.

D. no restrictions.

16. **Collaboration between the media specialist and classroom teacher is the key to an effective library media program. Which of the following scenarios best describes a media specialist willing to foster a collaborative partnership with a teacher?**
(Skill 1.6) Rigorous

A. The media specialist meets only when approached by a classroom teacher who is asking for help.

B. The media specialist can only meet on Tuesdays and Thursdays from 1-2 due to the fixed schedule that has been set up for the media center.

C. The media specialist touches base with teachers on a regular basis and attends grade level planning sessions.

D. The media specialist only meets with teachers on each grade level who are interested in working collaboratively.

17. When creating a schedule for a school library media center the type of schedule that maximizes access to resources is a:
(Skill 1.7) Easy

    A.   fixed schedule

    B.   open schedule

    C.   partial fixed schedule

    D.   flexible schedule

18. The TPRI is used to measure:
(Skill 1.7) Average rigor

    A.   Media program efficiency

    B.   Student reading proficiency

    C.   Media resource inventory

    D.   Student interests

19. After reading *The Pearl,* a tenth grader asks, "Why can't we start sentences with *and* like John Steinbeck?" This student is showing the ability to
(Skill 1.8) Rigorous

    A.   appreciate.

    B.   comprehend.

    C.   infer.

    D.   evaluate.

20. The first step in planning a training program for untrained support staff is
(Skills 1.8) Rigorous

    A.   assessing the employee's existing skills.

    B.   identifying and prioritizing skills from the job description/ evaluation instrument.

    C.   determining the time schedule for the completion of training.

    D.   studying the resume and speak to former employers.

21. Staff development activities in the use of materials and equipment are most effective if they
(Skills 1.8) Average Rigor

    A.   are conducted individually as need is expressed.

    B.   are sequenced in difficulty of operation or use.

    C.   result in use of the acquired skills in classroom lessons.

    D.   are evaluated for effectiveness.

22. **Which of the following is the most desirable learning outcome of a staff development workshop on *Teaching with Interactive DVDS*? Participants**
     (Skill 1.8) Average Rigor

   A.   score 80% or better on a post-test.

   B.   design content specific lessons from multiple resources.

   C.   sign up to take additional workshops.

   D.   encourage other teachers to participate in future workshops.

23. **A media specialist and classroom teacher are working collaboratively to develop activities that integrate technology into the curriculum. The best resource to use that ensures they are meeting state requirements would be:**
     (Skill 1.9) Average rigor

   A.   International Society for Technology in Education's National Educational Technology Standards

   B.   Texas Association for Educational Technology's Technology Standards

   C.   Texas Essential Knowledge and Skills

   D.   American Library Association's Curriculum Standards

24. **2x2 refers to:**
     (Skill 1.10) Easy

   A.   size of tables in a media center

   B.   space required for computer work station

   C.   a reading list for grades 2 through 4

   D.   A reading list for ages 2 through second grade

25. **All of the following are authors of young adult fiction EXCEPT**
(Skill 1.10) Rigorous

   A.   Paul Zindel.

   B.   Norma Fox Mazer.

   C.   S.E. Hinton.

   D.   Maurice Sendak.

26. **The award given for the best children's literature (text) is:**
(Skill 1.10) Easy

   A.   the Caldecott.

   B.   the Newbery.

   C.   the Pulitzer.

   D.   the Booklist.

27. **In recognition of outstanding translations of children's books this award was created in 1966. It is presented to the publisher that is responsible for translating the work into English.**
(Skill 1.10) Rigorous

   A.   Newberry Award.

   B.   Laura Ingalls Wilder Award.

   C.   Mildred L. Batchelder Award.

   D.   Carnegie Medal.

28. **This award was first presented to its namesake in 1954. This bronze medal award honors an author or illustrator whose books were published in the United States and have made a lasting contribution to literature for children. This award is known as the:**
(Skill 1.10) Rigorous

   A.   Newberry Award.

   B.   Laura Ingalls Wilder Award.

   C.   Mildred L. Batchelder Award.

   D.   Carnegie Medal.

29. **Contemporary library media design models should consider which of the following an optional need?**
(Skill 2.1) Rigorous

A. flexibility of space to allow for reading, viewing, and listening.

B. space for large group activities such as district meetings, standardized testing, and lectures.

C. traffic flow patterns for entrance and exit from the media center as well as easy movement within the center.

D. adequate and easy to rearrange storage areas for the variety of media formats and packaging style of modern materials.

30. **The most important consideration in the design of a new school library media center is**
(Skill 2.1) Average rigor

A. the goals of the library media center program.

B. the location of the facility on the school campus.

C. state standards for facilities use.

D. the demands of current technologies.

31. **When building or remodeling a media center which of the following is not an important design consideration?**
(Skill 2.2) Rigorous

A. The proximity of the media center to classrooms.

B. Traffic flow

C. Areas requiring supervision need to be readily visible.

D. Proper placement of electrical outlets, networking infrastructure, and security features.

32. Resources can be shared within a small geographic location such as a school by the use of a
(Skill 2.4) Average Rigor

  A.   SWN.

  B.   MAN.

  C.   LAN.

  D.   WAN.

33. All of the following are benefits of interlibrary loan except:
(Skill 2.4) Rigorous

  A.   maximizing the use media center funds.

  B.   providing a wider range of resources available for patrons.

  C.   building partnerships with outside agencies.

  D.   eliminating the need for media assistants.

34. A network allows which of the following to occur?
(Skill 2.4) Average Rigor

  A.   sharing files.

  B.   sharing printers.

  C.   sharing software.

  D.   all of the above

35. Factors that influence the atmosphere of a library media center contain all of the following except:
(Skill 2.5) Average rigor

  A.   aesthetic appearance

  B.   acoustical ceiling and floor coverings.

  C.   size of the media center

  D.   proximity to classrooms

36. The Position Statement on Flexible Scheduling was developed by :
(Skill 2.6) Rigorous

  A.   AASL

  B.   ALA

  C.   AECT

  D.   SLMA

37. A secondary school social studies teacher reads an article in the current month's *Smithsonian* that clarifies points in the unit of study on the day prior to the scheduled unit test. He asks the media specialist if copyright law would allow copying the entire 3100 word article for distribution to each student in his two honors American history classes. The media specialist's proper response is that
(Skill 2.6) Rigorous

A. he can make only one copy and read it to the class.

B. he may not copy it because of the word length.

C. he may excerpt sections of it to meet the brevity test.

D. he may copy the needed multiples, allowed by the spontaneity test.

38. Which of the following is an example of quantitative data that would be used to evaluate a school library media program?
(Skill 3.1) Average Rigor

A. Personnel evaluations

B. Usage statistics

C. Surveys

D. Interviews

39. An accredited elementary school has maintained an acceptable number of items in its print collection for ten years. In the evaluation review, this fact is evidence of both
(Skill 3.1) Rigorous

A. diagnostic and projective standards.

B. diagnostic and quantitative standards.

C. projective and quantitative standards.

D. projective and qualitative standards.

40. The principal is completing the annual report. He needs to include substantive data on use of the media center. In addition to the number of book circulations, he would like to know the proportionate use of the media center's facilities and services by the various grade levels or content areas. This information can most quickly be obtained from:
(Skill 3.1)Rigorous

   A. the class scheduling log.

   B. student surveys.

   C. lesson plans.

   D. inventory figures.

41. Lesson plans, Personnel evaluations, Surveys, Conferences, and Criterion-referenced or teacher made tests are forms of which standard
(Skill 3.1) Average rigor

   A. diagnostic standards.

   B. quantitative standards.

   C. projective standards.

   D. qualitative standards.

42. Ongoing evaluation is necessary to produce a quality media program. Use of evaluation results be used for all of the following except:
(Skill 3.1) Rigorous

   A. lobbying for budgetary or personnel support

   B. to make changes to the use of the media center materials

   C. to determine circulation regulations

   D. all of the above

43. Which of the following is the least effective way of communicating school library media policies, procedures, and rules to media center patrons?
(Skill 3.2) Average rigor

   A. announcements made in faculty and parent support group meetings.

   B. a published faculty procedures manual.

   C. written guidelines in the student handbook or special media handbill.

   D. a videotape orientation viewed over the school's closed circuit television system.

44. **Which of the following is a library policy, not a procedure?**
(*Skill 3.2*) *Rigorous*

   A.   providing a vehicle for the circulation of audio-visual equipment.

   B.   setting guidelines for collection development.

   C.   determining the method for introducing an objective into the school improvement plan.

   D.   setting categorical limits on operating expenses.

45. **A policy is:**
(*Skill 3.2*) *Easy*

   A.   a course of action taken to execute a plan.

   B.   a written statement of principle used to guarantee a management practice.

   C.   a statement of core values of an organization.

   D.   a regulation concerning certification.

46. **Which of the following should participate in the development of local policies and procedures:**
(*Skill 3.2*) *Average rigor*

   A.   teacher

   B.   student

   C.   parents

   D.   all of the above

47. **Policies that determine procedures for copyright laws and reproduction of materials are generally determined at which level:**
(*Skill 3.2*) *Average rigor*

   A.   grade level

   B.   school level

   C.   community level

   D.   district level

48. **In formulating an estimated collection budget consider all of the following except**
(*Skill 3.3*) *Rigorous*

   A.   attrition by loss, damage, or age.

   B.   the maximum cost of item replacement.

   C.   the number of students served.

   D.   the need for expansion to meet minimum guidelines.

49. **The most appropriate means of obtaining extra funds for library media programs is**
(Skill 3.3) Average rigor

  A. having candy sales.

  B. conducting book fairs.

  C. charging fines.

  D. soliciting donations.

50. **The two main categories of print resources found in most libraries are:**
(Skill 3.4) Average rigor

  A. reference and circulating materials

  B. picture books and chapter books

  C. reference books and picture books

  D. encyclopedias and chapter books

51. **All of the following are components of a circulation policy except:**
(Skill 3.4) Rigorous

  A. loan period

  B. process for handling overdues

  C. limitations

  D. location to post borrower's name

52. **The most efficient method of assessing which students are users or non-users of the library media center is reviewing**
(Skill 3.4) Average rigor

  A. patron circulation records.

  B. needs assessment surveys of students.

  C. monthly circulation statistics.

  D. the accession book for the current year.

53. **The procedures for conducting an inventory of the media collection include all of the following except:**
(Skill 3.4) Rigorous

  A. Determine the cost of the inventory.

  B. Determine when the inventory will be conducted.

  C. Determine who will conduct the inventory.

  D. Determine if each item matches the information in the holding records.

54. *AASL/AECT guidelines recommend that student library aides be* (Skill 3.5) *Average rigor*

    A. rewarded with grades or certificates for their service.

    B. allowed to assist only during free time.

    C. allowed to perform para- professional duties.

    D. assigned tasks that relate to maintaining the atmosphere of the media center.

55. **The most efficient method of evaluating support staff is to** (Skill 3.5) *Average rigor*

    A. administer a written test.

    B. survey faculty whom they serve.

    C. observe their performance.

    D. obtain verbal confirmation during an employee interview.

56. **According to *Information Power*, which of the following is NOT a responsibility of the school library media specialist?** (Skill 3.5) *Rigorous*

    A. maintaining and repairing equipment.

    B. instructing educators and parents in the use of library media resources.

    C. providing efficient retrieval systems for materials and equipment.

    D. planning and implementing the library media center budget.

57. **All of the following are areas in which the school library media specialist supports the learning community except** (Skill 3.5) *Average Rigor*

    A. Technician

    B. Collaboration

    C. Leadership

    D. Technology

58. **A school with 500 – 749 students should have how many media specialists?**
(Skill 3.5) Easy

   A.   1 part-time media specialist

   B.   1 full time media specialist

   C.   2 full time media specialist

   D.   no media specialist required

59. **Which of the following is the best description of the ALA recommendations for certification for a school library media specialist?**
(Skill 3.5) Easy

   A.   a bachelor's degree in any content area plus 30 hours of library/information science.

   B.   a master's degree from an accredited Educational Media progam.

   C.   a bachelor's degree in library/ information science and a master's degree in any field of education.

   D.   a master's degree from an accredited Library and Information Studies program.

60. **Which of these Dewey Decimal classifications should be weeded most often?**
(Skill 3.6) Rigorous

   A.   100s

   B.   500s

   C.   700s

   D.   Biographies

61. **The process of discarding worn or outdated books and materials is known as:**
(Skill 3.6) Easy

   A.   weeding

   B.   inventory

   C.   collection mapping

   D.   eliminating

62. **An acronym that is often used to remind media specialists of the steps to weeding a collection is:**
(Skill 3.6) Average rigor

   A.   WEAR

   B.   MUSTIE

   C.   ABCD

   D.   RIPPED

63. A policy that provides guidelines for the use of the school or district's electronic resources and the consequences that occur if the resources are not used properly.
(Skill 3.7) Easy

A. Collection development policy

B. Media selection policy

C. Acceptable use policy

D. None of the above

64. Automated circulation systems have all of the following advantages except:
(Skill 3.8) Average rigor

A. Require maintenance or original card catalog

B. Provide quick access to circulation statistics

C. Allow records to be searched easily

D. Provide quick access to all collection resources

65. A school library media specialist is searching for ways to make the school library more effective. Which of the following would not be a successful strategy?
(Skill 3.9) Rigorous

A. The school library media specialist develops activities that help to develop creativity and support critical thinking skills.

B. The school library media specialist works in isolation to plan effective programs that support curriculum guidelines.

C. The school library media specialist develops activities to expand students' interests and promote lifelong learning.

D. The school library media specialist provides physical access to resources.

66. A statement defining the core principles of a school library media program is called the:
(Skill 3.9) Average rigor

   A. mission

   B. policy

   C. procedure

   D. objective

67. The role of the Media Committee or Media Advisory Committee is to assist with all of the following except:
(Skill 3.9) Average rigor

   A. determine program direction

   B. evaluate the media specialist

   C. direct budget decisions

   D. collaborate with the media specialist

68. A general statement or outcome that is broken down into specific skills. This statement is known as a:
(Skill 3.9) Average rigor

   A. policy

   B. procedure

   C. goal

   D. objective

69. Long range plans should span how many years?
(Skill 16.1) Easy

   A. 2 – 4

   B. 3 – 5

   C. 5 – 10

   D. 10 – 15

70. School Library Programs: Standards and Guidelines for Texas, provides guidelines for exemplary media programs that include all of the following factors except:
(Skill 4.1) Average rigor

   A. Program evaluation occurs once per year.

   B. The program is student centered.

   C. A wide array of professional development is offered to meet individual needs.

   D. Parents are strongly encouraged to participate in learning activities.

71. **A media specialist is working to ensure that the media program is meeting the exemplary requirements as outlined by *School Library Programs: Standards and Guidelines for Texas*. Which of the following best describes such a program?**
(Skill 4.1) Rigorous

A. The media specialist has worked hard to find resources that meet curricular needs. There is adequate funding for building the collection. Even with her tightly fixed schedule the media specialist manages to meet with teachers occasionally. She has established a strong volunteer program to supplement the lack of adequate personnel.

B. The media specialist has created a student-centered program that focuses on strong collaboration with the classroom teacher. She constantly evaluates the program to ensure the resources available support the program and meets the needs of the students.

C. The media specialist collaborates with classroom teachers to ensure resources meet the needs of students. She has established partnerships within the community and a strong volunteer program to supplement the lack of adequate personnel.

D. The media specialist has created a student-centered program that focuses on strong collaboration with the classroom teacher. Time for planning has been built into the fixed schedule allowing her to integrate information skills and technology into weekly lessons.

72. Evaluation of a media program is crucial to its success. The data gathered during an evaluation can be beneficial for all of the following reasons except: *(Skill 4.2) Average rigor*

   A. The data can be beneficial during the budgeting process to determine priorities.

   B. Identifies weakness and strengths of the resource collection.

   C. Can assist with informing the community of the needs of the program.

   D. Provides an outline for staff responsibilities.

73. As a good leader, the media specialist must exhibit certain qualities and perform certain duties. These include all of the following except: *(Skill 4.3) Easy*

   A. Demonstrate appreciation for the work of others.

   B. Design and execute a media program on her own.

   C. Engage in continuing education.

   D. Maintain active memberships in professional organizations.

74. The American Library Association strongly advocates the use of the school library media program to address and celebrate the diverse populations within a school. There are simple ways a media program can address this topic:
(Skill 4.4) Average rigor

A. Provide resources that address a variety of cultures. This should include both fiction and non-fiction works.

B. Plan celebrations that focus upon various cultures or student populations.

C. Invite guest speakers related to these topics.

D. All of the above

75. Effective communication is essential to a quality media program. Which of the following is a benefit of effective communication?
(Skill 4.5) Average rigor

A. Allows the media specialist to convey the mission and goals

B. Allows the media specialist to convey current research

C. Provides the media specialist with the skills to prepare effective reports.

D. All of the above

76. Partners for a school library media program may include:
(Skills 4.6) Easy

A. universities

B. local businesses

C. community organizations

D. all of the above

77. **Parent involvement is critical to the support of a school and media program. Which of the following is the least effective way to increase parent involvement:**
(Skill 4.7)Easy

   A. Plan special family nights.

   B. Plan parent workshops

   C. Involve parents as volunteers.

   D. Send notes home to parents

78. **This outlines the role of the school library media specialist and the programs they manage.**
(Skill 4.8) Average Rigor

   A. Taxonomies of Learning

   B. Code of Ethics

   C. @ Your Library

   D. Library Bill of Rights

79. **Which version of *Information Power* was published in 1998?**
(Skill 5.1) Easy

   A. *Information Power: The Role of the School Library Media Program*

   B. *Information Power: A Review of Research*

   C. *Information Power: Guidelines for School Library Media Programs*

   D. *Information Power: Building Partnerships for Learning*

80. **All of the following organizations serve school libraries except:**
(Skill 5.1) Average Rigor

   A. AASL

   B. AECT

   C. ALCT

   D. ALA

81. National guidelines for school library media programs are generally developed by all of the following except: (Skill 5.1) Easy

    A. AASL

    B. ALA

    C. AECT

    D. NECT

82. School libraries have moved away from simply housing a collection of resources to serving as the central element of the school. The school library media program serves to provide students with the information they need to become lifelong learning.

    All are key factors that influence this role except: (Skill 5.2) Rigorous

    A. The development of a program that supports authentic learning experiences.

    B. The program must include accommodations for volunteers.

    C. Full administrative support.

    D. Effective integration of information literacy skills into the curriculum.

83. Which of the following is NOT one of three general criteria for selection of all materials? (Skill 5.3) Average rigor

    A. authenticity.

    B. appeal.

    C. appropriateness.

    D. allocation.

84. **Collection development policies are developed to accomplish all of the following except**
(Skill 5.3) Rigorous

   A. guarantee users freedom to access information.

   B. recognize the needs and interests of users.

   C. coordinate selection criteria and budget concerns.

   D. recognize rights of individuals or groups to challenge these policies.

85. **When selecting books for students in grades k-2, it is best to choose books with which of the following characteristics?**
(Skill 5.3) Easy

   A. strong picture support

   B. familiar language patterns

   C. utilize cuing systems

   D. all of the above

86. **MARC is the acronym for:**
(Skill 5.4) Easy

   A. Mobile Accessible Recorded Content

   B. Machine Accessible Readable Content

   C. Machine Readable Content

   D. Mobile Accessible Readable Content

87. **In MARC records the title information can be found under which tag?**
(Skill 5.4) Rigorous

   A. 130

   B. 245

   C. 425

   D. 520

88. **In which bibliographic field should information concerning the format of an audio-visual material appear? Rigor**
(Skill 5.5)

   A. Material specific details.

   B. Physical description.

   C. Notes.

   D. Standard numbers.

89. AACR2 is the acronym for: *(Skill 5.5) Easy*

    A.   Anglo-American Cataloging Rules Second Edition

    B.   American Association of Cataloging Rules Second Edition

    C.   American Association of Content Rules Second Edition

    D.   Anglo-American Content Rules Second Edition

90. OCLC is the acronym for: *(Skill 5.5) Average rigor*

    A.   Online Computer Library Center

    B.   Online Computer Library Catalog

    C.   Online Computer Library Conference

    D.   Online Computer Library Content

91. Which of the following is not a component of a bibliographic record? *(Skill 5.5) Rigorous*

    A.   Notes

    B.   Call number

    C.   Cover image

    D.   Physical description area

92. A periodical index search which allows the user to pair Keywords with <u>and</u>, <u>but</u>, or <u>or</u> is called *(Skill 5.6) Average Rigor*

    A.   Boolean.

    B.   dialoguing.

    C.   wildcarding.

    D.   truncation.

93. Which of the following searches would most likely return the most results? *(Skill 5.6) Average Rigor*

    A.   lions and tigers

    B.   lions not tigers

    C.   lions or tigers

    D.   lions and not tigers

94. A search that uses specific terms to locate information is called a:
    (Skill 5.6) Average rigor

    A.   reference search

    B.   keyword search

    C.   ready reference search

    D.   operator search

95. A request from a social studies for the creation of a list of historical fiction titles for a book report assignment is a _____ request.
    (Skill 5.7) Rigorous

    A.   ready reference.

    B.   research.

    C.   specific needs.

    D.   complex search.

96. When working with patrons to determine their specific information needs it may be necessary to ask the patron a series of questions that uncover needs, often called a:
    (Skill 5.7) Rigorous

    A.   ready reference request

    B.   special needs request

    C.   reference interview

    D.   evaluation interview

97. Which of the following would be a good question to ask during a reference interview?
    (Skill 5.7) Rigorous

    A.   Do you have a topic?

    B.   What is your topic?

    C.   Have you located any resources regarding your topic?

    D.   Do you know where to go to find the information?

98. All of the following are periodical directories except:
    (Skill 5.8) Average rigor

    A.   *Ulrich's*

    B.   *TNYT*

    C.   *SIRS*

    D.   *PAIS*

99. Which professional journal is published by the American Association of School Librarians?
    (Skill 5.8) Average rigor

    A.   *School Library Media Research*

    B.   *Library Trends*

    C.   *Library Power*

    D.   *Voices of Youth Advocate*

100. The program that is used to encourage students to read during the summer months is called:
(Skill 5.9) Easy

   A.   Texas Reading Club

   B.   Bluebonnet Reading Club

   C.   Lone Star Reading Club

   D.   None of the above

101. A student looks for a specific title on domestic violence. When he learns it is overdue, he asks the library media specialist to tell him the borrower's name. The library media specialist should first
(Skill 5.10) Rigorous

   A.   readily reveal the borrower's name.

   B.   suggest he look for the book in another library.

   C.   offer to put the boy's name on reserve pending the book's return.

   D.   offer to request an interlibrary loan.

102. The Right to Read Statement was issued by:
(Skill 5.10) Rigorous

   A.   AECT

   B.   ALA

   C.   NCTE

   D.   NICEM

103. All of the following are state library and technology organizations except:
(Skill 5.11) Average rigor

   A.   TCEA

   B.   TAET

   C.   TLA

   D.   TASL

104. Which of the following is not a national organization that supports media and technology efforts:
(Skill 5.11) Rigorous

   A.   NCTM

   B.   ALA

   C.   AASL

   D.   ASCD

105. Which of the following file extensions does not represent an image file?
(Skill 6.1) Average Rigor

   A.   .jpeg

   B.   .gif

   C.   .csv

   D.   .bmp

106. A group of students in the business club will be creating a website to sell their product. When selecting their domain name, which of the following extensions would be best to use?
(Skill 6.1) Rigorous

   A.   .com

   B.   .edu

   C.   .cfm

   D.   .html

107. Which of the following is not a criterion used to evaluate resources for a media collection?
(Skill 6.2) Easy

   A.   Audience

   B.   Scope

   C.   Accuracy

   D.   All of the above

108. Instruction provided via satellite or cable television is called
(Skill 6.3) Average Rigor

   A.   home study.

   B.   distance learning.

   C.   extension services.

   D.   telecommunications.

109. Advantages of distance education include all of the following except:
(Skill 6.3) Rigorous

   A.   students can access and respond to information outside of a normal schedule.

   B.   students have fewer choices regarding content.

   C.   homebound students may receive instruction.

   D.   it may be more cost effective to use distance learning than to hire a teacher.

110. When allowing interlibrary loan with a public library, which item should be taken into consideration?
(Skill 6.4) Rigorous

  A.   Where the item will be housed?

  B.   How will funds be distributed?

  C.   How personnel will be distributed.

  D.   None of the above

111. Web page editing software that allows the user to preview web pages as they are being created is called:
(Skill 6.5) Average rigor

  A.   WYSWYG

  B.   WYSIYG

  C.   WISWYG

  D.   WYSIWYG

112. Software designed to organize, manage and retrieve resources quickly and easily is called:
(Skill 6.5) Average rigor

  A.   database

  B.   spreadsheet

  C.   word processing

  D.   teleconference

113. Software that allows users to communicate over the Internet using audio and/or video is called:
(Skill 6.5) Rigorous

  A.   database

  B.   spreadsheet

  C.   web editor

  D.   teleconferencing

114. Texas Essential Knowledge and Skills (TEKS) stress the importance of integrating information and technology skills to assist with problem-solving processes. There are three main areas where technology works with this process. Which is not an example?
(Skill 6.6) Rigorous

  A.   Use appropriate technology to modify the solution to problems.

  B.   Use technology to communicate with others and enhance research skills.

  C.   Use technology to locate and use information.

  D.   Use technology to evaluate both the process and product of information learned.

115. The media specialist is searching a database and needs to locate all of the entries that begin with the letter "P". What is the best way to format this search?
(Skill 6.7) Rigorous

    A.   Create a search using the Boolean operator AND NOT. (P AND NOT A, B, C, D, E…)

    B.   Place quotations around the letter P

    C.   Use a wildcard

    D.   This type of search cannot be done.

116. In the production of a teacher/student made audio-visual material, which of the following is NOT a factor in the planning phase?
(Skill 6.8) Rigorous

    A.   stating the objectives.

    B.   analyzing the audience.

    C.   determining the purpose.

    D.   selecting the format.

117. Which of the following formats is best for large group presentations?
(Skill 6.8) Easy

    A.   manipulatives

    B.   multimedia

    C.   audio recordings

    D.   photographs

118. All of the following formats are best for small group learning except:
(Skill 6.8) Average rigor

    A.   manipulatives

    B.   computer projection

    C.   photographs

    D.   computer software

119. The school library media specialist is responsible for helping to prepare students to be 21st century citizen. An important part of this process is to stay abreast of the technology initiatives at various levels. All of the following can assist with this process except:
(Skill 6.9) Average rigor

   A. subscribing to newsletters

   B. sending newsletters to staff

   C. participating in library related discussion boards

   D. actively participating in state and national library associations

120. The acronym OPAC stands for:
(Skill 6.10) Average rigor

   A. Online Public Access Catalogs

   B. Organization for Public Accessible Catalogs

   C. Online Patron Accessible Catalogs

   D. Organization for Public Access Catalogs

121. In a school with one full-time library media assistant (clerk), which of the following are responsibilities of the assistant?
(Skill 3.5) Average rigor

   A. selecting and ordering titles for the print collection.

   B. performing circulation tasks and processing new materials.

   C. inservicing teachers on the integration of media materials into the school curriculum.

   D. planning and implementing programs to involve parents and community

122. Which periodical contains book reviews of currently published children and young adult books?
(Skill 5.8) Rigorous

   A. Phi Delta Kappan

   B. School Library Journal

   C. School Library Media Quarterly

   D. American Teacher

123. It is often necessary that equipment be shared amongst teachers. The equipment can be checked out from the media center. Which of the following is necessary for the use and transporting of equipment?
(Skill 3.4) Rigorous

A.   Directions for use

B.   Straps or lock-downs to secure items being transported

C.   Having a staff member on hand to assist with set up.

D.   None of the above.

124. Collaborative partnerships with staff can take on many forms. All of the following are examples except:
(Skill 3.9) Rigorous

A.   serving on curriculum development committees

B.   viewing the school's curriculum and creating lessons

C.   assisting teachers in planning, designing, and teaching lessons

D.   assisting teachers and students with the use of new technologies

125. When implementing new technologies it is important for the media specialist to model its use. It is also important for the media specialist to:
(Skill 6.7) Average rigor

A.   Send updated hand-outs to staff.

B.   Provide web resources to assist with utilization of the tool.

C.   Provide brief refresher modules.

D.   All of the above.

Answer Key

1.	D	33.	D	65.	B	97.	B
2.	C	34.	D	66.	A	98.	B
3.	C	35.	C	67.	B	99.	A
4.	B	36.	A	68.	C	100.	A
5.	C	37.	D	69.	B	101.	C
6.	B	38.	B	70.	A	102.	C
7.	C	39.	B	71.	B	103.	B
8.	C	40.	A	72.	D	104.	A
9.	C	41.	D	73.	B	105.	C
10.	A	42.	D	74.	D	106.	A
11.	D	43.	A	75.	D	107.	D
12.	A	44.	B	76.	D	108.	B
13.	B	45.	B	77.	D	109.	B
14.	B	46.	D	78.	C	110.	D
15.	C	47.	D	79.	D	111.	D
16.	B	48.	B	80.	C	112.	A
17.	D	49.	B	81.	D	113.	D
18.	B	50.	A	82.	B	114.	C
19.	D	51.	D	83.	D	115.	C
20.	B	52.	A	84.	C	116.	D
21.	C	53.	A	85.	D	117.	B
22.	B	54.	A	86.	C	118.	D
23.	C	55.	C	87.	B	119.	B
24.	D	56.	A	88.	C	120.	A
25.	D	57.	A	89.	A	121.	B
26.	B	58.	B	90.	A	122.	B
27.	C	59.	D	91.	C	123.	B
28.	C	60.	B	92.	A	124.	B
29.	B	61.	A	93.	C	125.	D
30.	A	62.	B	94.	B		
31.	A	63.	C	95.	C		
32.	C	64.	A	96.	C		

Rigor Table

Easy –   1, 5, 17, 24, 26, 45, 58, 59, 61, 63, 69, 73, 76, 77, 79, 84, 85, 86, 89, 100, 107, 117

Average Rigor -   2, 4, 6, 7, 10, 14, 18, 21, 22, 23, 30, 32, 34, 35, 38, 41, 43, 46, 47, 49, 50, 52, 54, 55, 57, 62, 64, 66, 67, 68, 70, 72, 74, 75, 78, 80, 83, 90, 92, 93, 94, 98, 99, 103, 105, 108, 111, 112, 118, 119, 120, 121, 125

Rigorous-   3, 8, 9, 11, 12, 13, 15, 16, 19, 20, 25, 27, 28, 29, 31, 33, 36, 36, 39, 40, 42, 44, 48, 51, 53, 56, 60, 65, 71, 82, 84, 87, 88, 91, 95, 96, 97, 101, 102, 104, 106, 109, 110, 113, 114, 115, 116, 122, 123, 124

Answers with Rationale

1. **A good leader should:**
   (Skill 1.1) Easy

   a. delegate responsibility
   b. show respect for colleagues
   c. engage in continuing education
   d. all of the above

Answer: d. all of the above

A good leader should strive to continuously improve their performance while building a great team to accomplish the desired goal. It is important that the demonstrate their quest to be a lifelong learner, respect their colleagues and learn to delegate responsibilities based upon the strengths of those around them.

2. **The English I (9th Grade) teacher wants his students to become familiar with the contents of books in the reference area of the school library media center. He asks the library media specialist to recommend an activity to accomplish this goal. Which of the following activities would best achieve the goal?**
   (Skill 1.2) Average Rigor

   a. Assign a research paper on a specific social issues topic.
   b. Require a biography of a famous person.
   c. Design a set of questions covering a variety of topics and initiate a scavenger hunt approach to their location.
   d. Teach students the Dewey Decimal system and have them list several books in each Dewey subcategory.

Answer: c. Design a set of questions covering a variety of topics and initiate a scavenger hunt approach to their location.

Students often learn best by doing. If the teacher's goal was for students to learn to use reference materials, then the best way to accomplish this is to design a task that does just that. In this case the students are applying their knowledge making Option C the best answer.

3. **The TAXONOMIES OF THE SCHOOL LIBRARY MEDIA PROGRAM outlines eleven levels of school library media specialists' involvement with curriculum and instruction and was developed by:**
    (Skill 1.3) Rigorous

a. Eisenberg.
b. Bloom.
c. Loertscher.
d. Lance.

Answer: c. Loertscher

Eisenberg is one of the creators of the Big 6 Model. Bloom was the developer of Bloom's Taxonomy. Keith Curry-Lance has conducted many studies on the effect of school library media programs on student achievement.

4. **The school library media center should be an inviting space that encourages learning. To accomplish this the school library media specialist should do all of the following except:**
    (Skill 1.3) Average rigor

a. collaborate with school staff and students.
b. create a schedule where each class comes to the media center each eek for instruction.
c. arrange materials so that they are easy to locate.
d. promote the program as a wonderful place for learning.

Answer: b. create a schedule where each class comes to the media center each week for instruction

The goal of a school library is to operate under a flexible schedule to maximize use of the media center and its resources. This makes Option B the most appropriate answer.

5.   **To foster the collaborative process the media specialist must possess all of the following skills except:**
      (Skill 1.3) Easy

a.   leadership
b.   flexibility
c.   perverse
d.   persistence

Answer: c. be perverse

A school library media specialist must be flexible, possess good leadership skills, and be persistent making Option C the most appropriate response.

6.   **A cooperative relationship between a media specialist and a teacher is known as:**
      (Skill 4.5) Average rigor

a.   collection development
b.   collaboration
c.   telecommunications
d.   flexible scheduling

Answer: b. collaboration

The most appropriate answer is Option B. The cooperative relationship between a media specialist and a teacher is known as collaboration.

7.   The media specialist is interested in beginning collaborative planning sessions with the teachers within the school, but not all of the teachers are interested. The media specialist should: *(Skill 9.3) Average rigor*

a.   wait until all of the teachers are interested
b.   have the principal make all teachers collaboratively plan with the media specialist
c.   work with the teachers who are most willing to engage in the process
d.   abandon the idea

Answer: c. work with the teachers who are most willing to engage in the process

A good place for media specialists to begin forming collaborative relationships is with those who are willing. As the media specialist gains confidence and support they need to branch out to meet with all teachers. Planning with teachers during grade level meetings is an ideal way to enhance the process.

8.   Steps in the Big6 Model include all of the following except: *(Skill 1.4) Rigorous*

a.   information seeking strategies
b.   location and access
c.   creation of information
d.   task definition

Answer: c. creation of information

Creation of information is the only option that is not included in the Big6 Information Literacy model. Option C is the most appropriate answer.

9. **Another popular information literacy model is:**
    (Skill 1.4) Rigorous

a. Bloom's Taxonomies
b. Star Reader
c. Pathways to Knowledge
d. Follett Taxonomies

Answer: c. Pathways to Knowledge

Pathways to Knowledge is an information literacy model that closely follows the steps outlined in the Big 6 model. Option C is the most appropriate answer.

10. **The creators of the Big 6 Model are:**
    (Skill 1.4) Average Rigor

a. Eisenberg and Berkowitz.
b. Marzano and Bloom.
c. Bloom and Gardner.
d. Lance and Eisenberg.

Answer: a. Eisenberg and Berkowitz

The correct answer is Option A. Mike Eisenberg and Bob Berkowitz are the creators of the Big 6 Model for developing Information Literacy Skills.

11. **A secondary school social studies teacher reads an article in the current month's *Smithsonian* that clarifies points in the unit of study on the day prior to the scheduled unit test. He asks the media specialist if copyright law would allow copying the entire 3100 word article for distribution to each student in his two honors American history classes. The media specialist's proper response is that**
    (Skill 1.5) Rigorous

a. he can make only one copy and read it to the class.
b. he may not copy it because of the word length.
c. he may excerpt sections of it to meet the brevity test.
d. he may copy the needed multiples, allowed by the spontaneity test.

Answer: d. He may copy the needed multiples, allowed by the spontaneity test.

Fair Use guidelines for nonprofit educational organizations does allow the copying and use of an entire article if it meets either the brevity or spontaneity test.

12. **Section 108 of the Copyright Act permits the copying of an entire book if three conditions are met. Which of the following is NOT one of those conditions?**
    (Skill 1.5) Rigorous

a.   The library intends to allow inter- library loan of the book.
b.   The library is an archival library.
c.   The copyright notice appears on all the copies.
d.   The library is a public library.

Answer: a. The library intends to allow inter-library loan of the book.

Section 108 does allow a library to make a single copy of a book for archival purposes. It does not cover books that are to be copied and used for inter-library loans.

13. **Under the copyright brevity test, an educator may reproduce without written permission**
    (Skill 1.5) Rigorous

a.   10% of any prose or poetry work.
b.   500 words from a 5000 word article.
c.   240 words of a 2400 word story.
d.   no work over 2500 words.

Answer: b. 500 words from a 5000 word article.

Under the brevity test up to 250 words of a poem can be copied providing it is under 2 pages. An article of 2500 words or less can be copied entirely. Ten percent of an article over 2500 words can be used making Option B the most appropriate answer.

14. **Licensing has become a popular means of copyright protection in the area of**
(Skill 1.5) Average Rigor

a. duplicating books for interlibrary loan.
b. use of software application on multiple machines.
c. music copying.
d. making transparency copies of books or workbooks that are too expensive to purchase.

Answer: b. Use of software application on multiple machines.

When purchasing software the customer will generally received either a CD-ROM or DVD for installation purposes. The most important piece of packaging or file included on the software is the license. The license(s) purchased determine the number of computers in which the software can be loaded. Installing the software on more than the number listed on the license violated copyright and can result in a lawsuit by the publisher.

15. **"Fair Use" policy in videotaping off-air from commercial television requires**
(Skill 1.5) Rigorous

a. show in 5 days, erase by the 20th day.
b. show in 10 days, erase by the 30th day.
c. show in 10 days, erase by the 45th day.
d. no restrictions.

Answer: c. Show in 10 days, erase by the 45th day.

Fair Use Guidelines for recorded videotapes for nonprofit educational institutions state that the recording must be shown within 10 days and must be erased by the 45th day.

16. Collaboration between the media specialist and classroom teacher is the key to an effective library media program. Which of the following scenarios best describes a media specialist willing to foster a collaborative partnership with a teacher?
(Skill 1.6) Rigorous

a. The media specialist meets only when approached by a classroom teacher who is asking for help.
b. The media specialist can only meet on Tuesdays and Thursdays from 1-2 due to the fixed schedule that has been set up for the media center.
c. The media specialist touches base with teachers on a regular basis and attends grade level planning sessions.
d. The media specialist only meets with teachers on each grade level who are interested in working collaboratively.

Answer: b. The media specialist can only meet on Tuesdays and Thursdays from 1-2 due to the fixed schedule that has been set up for the media center.

A flexible schedule is most conducive to fostering the collaborative process with teachers. When a media specialist is on a fixed schedule and only has a limited time each week to plan with teachers, the media specialist loses some of their effectiveness. Option B is the most appropriate answer.

17. When creating a schedule for a school library media center the type of schedule that maximizes access to resources is a:
(Skill 1.7) Easy

a. fixed schedule
b. open schedule
c. partial fixed schedule
d. flexible schedule

Answer: d. flexible schedule
The best answer is d, flexible schedule. A flexible schedule allows students to have access to resources at the point of need. It maximizes the use of resources and allows media specialists to be accessible for collaborative planning with teachers.

18.   The TPRI is used to measure:
(Skill 1.7) Average rigor

a.   Media program efficiency
b.   Student reading proficiency
c.   Media resource inventory
d.   Student interests

Answer: b. Student reading proficiency

The TPRI is the acronym for the Texas Primary Reading Inventory. This inventory is used to measure reading progress throughout the school year. Option B is the most appropriate answer.

19.   After reading *The Pearl,* a tenth grader asks, "Why can't we start sentences with *and* like John Steinbeck?" This student is showing the ability to
(Skill 1.8) Rigorous

a.   appreciate.
b.   comprehend.
c.   infer.
d.   evaluate.

Answer: d. evaluate.

Under the description of the Bloom's Taxonomy level of evaluation students that demonstrate this level of higher order thinking are able to :
- Make choices based upon well thought out arguments
- Compare ideas
- And recognize subjectivity

20. **The first step in planning a training program for untrained support staff is**
    (Skills 1.8) Rigorous

a. assessing the employee's existing skills.
b. identifying and prioritizing skills from the job description/ evaluation instrument.
c. determining the time schedule for the completion of training.
d. studying the resume and speak to former employers.

Answer: b. Identifying and prioritizing skills from the job description/ evaluation instrument.

The best place to begin planning a training program for untrained support staff is to take a look at the job description or evaluation instrument and determine the skills that need to be learned. From there one could study the employee's resume, assess their skills and plan a schedule for training

21. **Staff development activities in the use of materials and equipment are most effective if they**
    (Skills 1.8) Average Rigor

a. are conducted individually as need is expressed.
b. are sequenced in difficulty of operation or use.
c. result in use of the acquired skills in classroom lessons.
d. are evaluated for effectiveness.

Answer: c. Result in use of the acquired skills in classroom lessons.

Option C is the most appropriate answer. The ultimate goal of most staff development activities is use or integration in the classroom.

22. **Which of the following is the most desirable learning outcome of a staff development workshop on *Teaching with Interactive DVDS*? Participants**
(Skill 1.8) Average Rigor

a. score 80% or better on a post- test.
b. design content specific lessons from multiple resources.
c. sign up to take additional workshops.
d. encourage other teachers to participate in future workshops.

Answer: b. Design content specific lessons from multiple resources.

The purpose of most staff development workshops is to foster integration of resources into the classroom. Performance and attendance in future workshops is desirable, but not the main goal.

23. **A media specialist and classroom teacher are working collaboratively to develop activities that integrate technology into the curriculum. The best resource to use that ensures they are meeting state requirements would be:**
(Skill 1.9) Average rigor

a. International Society for Technology in Education's National Educational Technology Standards
b. Texas Association for Educational Technology's Technology Standards
c. Texas Essential Knowledge and Skills
d. American Library Association's Curriculum Standards

Answer: c. Texas Essential Knowledge and Skills

It is important that integrated lessons focus on the content found in the Texas Essential Knowledge and Skills. The most appropriate answer is Option C.

24.   **2x2 refers to:**
        (Skill 1.10) Easy

a.   size of tables in a media center
b.   space required for computer work station
c.   a reading list for grades 2 through 4
d.   a reading list for ages 2 through second grade

Answer: d. a reading list for ages 2 through second grade

2x2 is the Texas reading list fro ages two through second grade. Other reading lists include:
*   The Texas Bluebonnet Award for grades 3- 6 allows students to vote on their favorite book from a select list. To vote, a student must read at least five of the books on the list.
*   The Lone Star list is a reading list for grades 6 – 8.
*   The Tayshus list is a reading list for high schoolers

25.   **All of the following are authors of young adult fiction EXCEPT**
        (Skill 1.10) Rigorous

a.   Paul Zindel.
b.   Norma Fox Mazer.
c.   S.E. Hinton.
d.   Maurice Sendak.

Answer: d. Maurice Sendak

Maurice Sendak is best know for his picture books for young children such as *Where the Wild Things Are*.

26.   **The award given for the best children's literature (text) is:**
        (Skill 1.10) Easy

a.   the Caldecott.
b.   the Newbery.
c.   the Pulitzer.
d.   the Booklist.

Answer: b. the Newbery

Option B, the Newbery Award, is the award give to an outstanding children's book. It was named for bookseller John Newbery, who was the first to publish literature for children in the second half of 18th century England. While the Caldecott Award does recognize children's literature, this award is for outstanding illustrators.

27. **In recognition of outstanding translations of children's books this award was created in 1966. It is presented to the publisher that is responsible for translating the work into English.**
(Skill 1.10) Rigorous

a. Newberry Award.
b. Laura Ingalls Wilder Award.
c. Mildred L. Batchelder Award.
d. Carnegie Medal.

Answer: c. Mildred L. Batchelder Award
The most appropriate answer is Option C. The Batchelder Award was first presented in 1966 to the American publisher of a book first published in a foreign language. The Newberry Award honors the author who has made the most distinguished contribution to children's literature. The Carnegie Medal is an award for excellence in children's videos.

28. **This award was first presented to its namesake in 1954. This bronze medal award honors an author or illustrator whose books were published in the United States and have made a lasting contribution to literature for children. This award is known as the:**
(Skill 1.10) Rigorous

a. Newberry Award.
b. Laura Ingalls Wilder Award.
c. Mildred L. Batchelder Award.
d. Carnegie Medal.

Answer: c. Laura Ingalls Wilder Award

The most appropriate answer is Option B, the Laura Ingalls Wilder Award. The Newberry Award honors the author who has made the most distinguished contribution to children's literature. The Batchelder Award was first presented in 1966 to the American publisher of a book first published in a foreign language. The Carnegie Medal is an award for excellence in children's videos.

29. **Contemporary library media design models should consider which of the following an optional need?**
(Skill 2.1) Rigorous

a. flexibility of space to allow for reading, viewing, and listening.
b. space for large group activities such as district meetings, standardized testing, and lectures.
c. traffic flow patterns for entrance and exit from the media center as well as easy movement within the center.
d. adequate and easy to rearrange storage areas for the variety of media formats and packaging style of modern materials.

Answer: b. space for large group activities such as district meetings, standardized testing, and lectures.

Flexibility of space, traffic flow patterns that allow ease of movement, and adequate storage are all crucial to design of a media center. Therefore, Option B is the best answer. While a space for large group activities is desirable for community use, it is not vital to the operation of a school library media center.

30. **The most important consideration in the design of a new school library media center is**
(Skill 2.1) Average Rigor

a. the goals of the library media center program.
b. the location of the facility on the school campus.
c. state standards for facilities use.
d. the demands of current technologies.

Answer: a. the goals of the library media center program

The goals of a library media program should be a most important consideration when planning a new school media center. The other options should be considered, but Option A is the most appropriate answer.

31. **When building or remodeling a media center which of the following is not an important design consideration?**
(Skill 2.2) Rigorous

a. The proximity of the media center to classrooms.
b. Traffic flow
c. Areas requiring supervision need to be readily visible.
d. Proper placement of electrical outlets, networking infrastructure, and security features.

Answer: a. The proximity of the media center to classrooms.

When designing a media center all but Option A are important considerations. Traffic flow through various areas is a necessary consideration. It is important to make sure all areas are visible for supervision. Placement of outlets, networking equipment and security features must be determined to ensure all areas are properly equipped.

32. **Resources can be shared within a small geographic location such as a school by the use of a**
(Skill 2.4) Average Rigor

a. SWN.
b. MAN.
c. LAN.
d. WAN.

Answer: c. LAN

A LAN or local area network allows users to share information within a small geographic area. The WAN or wide area network allows users to share information over a large geographic area.

33. **All of the following are benefits of interlibrary loan except:**
(Skill 2.4) Rigorous

a. maximizing the use media center funds.
b. providing a wider range of resources available for patrons.
c. building partnerships with outside agencies.
d. eliminating the need for media assistants.

Answer: d. eliminating the need for media assistants

The most appropriate response is Option D. Interlibrary loan allows the cooperating entities to maximize both funds and resources. It does not eliminate the need for media assistants.

34. **A network allows which of the following to occur?**
    (Skill 2.4) Average Rigor

a.   sharing files.
b.   sharing printers.
c.   sharing software.
d.   all of the above

Answer: d. all of the above.

A network allows the sharing of files, printers, and software. This makes Option D the most appropriate response.

35. **Factors that influence the atmosphere of a library media center contain all of the following except:**
    (Skill 2.5) Average rigor

a.   aesthetic appearance
b.   acoustical ceiling and floor coverings.
c.   size of the media center
d.   proximity to classrooms

Answer: c. size of the media center

While the size of the media center is important, it does not necessarily have a bearing on the atmosphere. This makes Option C the most appropriate answer.

36. **The Position Statement on Flexible Scheduling was developed by:**
    (Skill 2.6) *Rigorous*

a.   AASL
b.   ALA
c.   AECT
d.   SLMA

Answer: a. AASL

The American Association of School Librarians have issued the Position Statement on Flexible Scheduling. It recommends full integration of information skills into the curriculum. Option A is the most appropriate answer.

37.   A secondary school social studies teacher reads an article in the current month's *Smithsonian* that clarifies points in the unit of study on the day prior to the scheduled unit test. He asks the media specialist if copyright law would allow copying the entire 3100 word article for distribution to each student in his two honors American history classes. The media specialist's proper response is that *(Skill 2.6) Rigorous*

a.   he can make only one copy and read it to the class.
b.   he may not copy it because of the word length.
c.   he may excerpt sections of it to meet the brevity test.
d.   he may copy the needed multiples, allowed by the spontaneity test.

Answer: d. He may copy the needed multiples, allowed by the spontaneity test.

Fair Use guidelines for nonprofit educational organizations does allow the copying and use of an entire article if it meets either the brevity or spontaneity test.

38.   Which of the following is an example of quantitative data that would be used to evaluate a school library media program? *(Skill 3.1) Average Rigor*

a.   Personnel evaluations
b.   Usage statistics
c.   Surveys
d.   Interviews

Answer b. Usage statistics

Option B is the most appropriate answer because it is the only one listed that provides measurable data. All of the others are qualitative forms of data.

39.   An accredited elementary school has maintained an acceptable
      number of items in its print collection for ten years. In the evaluation
      review, this fact is evidence of both
      (Skill 3.1) Rigorous

a.   diagnostic and projective standards.
b.   diagnostic and quantitative standards.
c.   projective and quantitative standards.
d.   projective and qualitative standards.

Answer: b. diagnostic and quantitative standards.

Diagnostic evaluations are standards based on conditions existing in programs
that have already been judged excellent. The acceptable print collection can be
compared to national guidelines for diagnostic information. Quantitative
evaluations involve numerical data of some kind. By taking a look at the
numbers in the collection the media specialist can review collection totals.
Option B is the correct answer.

40.   The principal is completing the annual report. He needs to include
      substantive data on use of the media center. In addition to the
      number of book circulations, he would like to know the proportionate
      use of the media center's facilities and services by the various grade
      levels or content areas. This information can most quickly be
      obtained from:
      (Skill 3.1) Rigorous

a.   the class scheduling log.

b.   student surveys.

c.   lesson plans.

d.   inventory figures.

Answer: a. the class scheduling log

One of the best tools to use to determine how the media center's facilities are
being used is the schedule. Often the schedule is broken down by the various
areas in the media center. Teachers may schedule the specific area(s) they
need. This makes Option A the most appropriate answer.

41. **Lesson plans, personnel evaluations, surveys, conferences, and criterion-referenced or teacher made tests are forms of which standard**
     (Skill 3.2) Average rigor

a.   diagnostic standards.
b.   quantitative standards.
c.   projective standards.
d.   qualitative standards.

Answer: d. qualitative standards

Qualitative standards are descriptive in nature. Alll of the items listed are forms of qualitative data. This makes Option D the most appropriate answer.

42. **Ongoing evaluation is necessary to produce a quality media program. Use of evaluation results be used for all of the following except:**
     (Skill 3.1) Rigorous

a.   lobbying for budgetary or personnel support
b.   to make changes to the use of the media center materials
c.   to determine circulation regulations
d.   all of the above

Answer: D. all of the above

Evaluating a media program can be very beneficial. It can assist the media specialist in justifying budget requests, making changes to the media center resources, and determine circulation regulations. Option D is the most appropriate answer.

43. **Which of the following is the least effective way of communicating school library media policies, procedures, and rules to media center patrons?**
(Skill 3.2) Average Rigor

a. announcements made in faculty and parent support group meetings.
b. a published faculty procedures manual.
c. written guidelines in the student handbook or special media handbill.
d. a videotaped orientation viewed over the school's closed circuit television system.

Answer: a. announcements made in faculty and parent support group meetings.

When providing information regarding policies, procedures and rules for media center patrons it is important to provide them with tangible and detailed information. With Option A, announcements at meetings, the information is not necessarily written down and the media specialist may have to rely on those present to share information with others. It is the least reliable.

44. **Which of the following is a library policy, not a procedure?**
(Skill 3.2) Rigorous

a. providing a vehicle for the circulation of audio-visual equipment.
b. setting guidelines for collection development.
c. determining the method for introducing an objective into the school improvement plan.
d. setting categorical limits on operating expenses.

Answer: b. setting guidelines for collection development.

A policy is a plan or a course of action such as setting the guidelines for collection development as listed in Option B. A procedure is a set of specific steps or methods used to perform a specific action.

45.   A policy is:
      (Skill 3.2) *Easy*

a.   a course of action taken to execute a plan.
b.   a written statement of principle used to guarantee a management practice.
c.   a statement of core values of an organization.
d.   a regulation concerning certification.

Answer: b. a course of action taken to execute a plan.

The most appropriate answer was Option A. A procedure is a course of action taken to execute a plan. A mission is a statement of core values.

46.   Which of the following should participate in the development of local policies and procedures:
      (*Skill 3.2*) *Average rigor*

a.   teacher
b.   student
c.   parents
d.   all of the above

Answer: d. all of the above

Teachers, students and parents should play a role in the development of local policies and procedures. This ensures equity for all types of users and gains insight from differing viewpoints. Administrators and media specialists should also serve on such a committee.

47.   Policies that determine procedures for copyright laws and reproduction of materials are generally determined at which level:
      (*Skill 16.3*) *Average rigor*

a.   grade level
b.   school level
c.   community level
d.   district level

Answer: d. District level

Policies regarding copyright and acceptable use of resources are generally created at the district level. Individual schools may adopt extra requirements, but the overall guidelines are set on a larger scale.

48.   **In formulating an estimated collection budget consider all of the following except**
       (Skill 3.3) Rigorous

a.   attrition by loss, damage, or age.
b.   the maximum cost of item replacement.
c.   the number of students served.
d.   the need for expansion to meet minimum guidelines.

Answer: b. the maximum cost of item replacement

The first consideration for formulating a collection budget is to determine whether or not the collection meets minimum guidelines. Then decide upon the funding needed to meet the guidelines. It is also important to allot funds to replace lost or worn items. Option B, the maximum cost of item replacement is not used in formulating a collection budget making it the most appropriate answer.

49.   **The most appropriate means of obtaining extra funds for library media programs is**
       (Skill 3.3) Average rigor

a.   having candy sales.
b.   conducting book fairs.
c.   charging fines.
d.   soliciting donations.

Answer: b. conducting book fairs.

The most appropriate answer for this question is Option B, conducting book fairs. This keeps in line with the main focus of a school library media program, literacy.

50.   **The two main categories of print resources found in most libraries are:**
       (Skill 3.4) Average rigor

a.   reference and circulating materials
b.   picture books and chapter books
c.   reference books and picture books
d.   encyclopedias and chapter books

Answer: a. reference and circulating materials

Materials in a media collection are generally found under two main headings, reference and circulating materials. Reference materials normally stay in the media center or are reserved under special check-out. Circulating materials are all of those that are checked out for patron use.

51.   **All of the following are components of a circulation policy except:**
      (Skill 3.4) Rigorous

a.   loan period
b.   process for handling overdues
c.   limitations
d.   location to post borrower's name

Answer: d. location to post borrower's name

The location to post a borrower's name is not a part of a circulation policy. The policy should include the length of the loan period, how to handle overdues, and such limitations as the number of books that can be checked out at once.

52.   **The most efficient method of assessing which students are users or non-users of the library media center is reviewing**
      (Skill 3.4) Average rigor

a.   patron circulation records.
b.   needs assessment surveys of students.
c.   monthly circulation statistics.
d.   the accession book for the current year.

Answer: a. patron circulation records.

By reviewing circulation records the school library media specialists can quickly survey who is and isn't checking out materials making Option A the best answer. A needs assessment generally takes a good deal of time to complete. The monthly circulation records provide a snapshot of the number of books checked out during a specific period.

53.   **The procedures for conducting an inventory of the media collection include all of the following except:**
      (Skill 3.4) Rigorous

a.   Determine the cost of the inventory.
b.   Determine when the inventory will be conducted.
c.   Determine who will conduct the inventory.
d.   Determine if each item matches the information in the holding records.

Answer: a. Determine the cost of the inventory.

When conducting an inventory it is not necessary to determine the cost of the inventory. Option A is the most appropriate answer.

54.   *AASL/AECT guidelines recommend that student library aides be (Skill 3.5) Average Rigor*

a.   rewarded with grades or certificates for their service.
b.   allowed to assist only during free time.
c.   allowed to perform paraprofessional duties.
d.   assigned tasks that relate to maintaining the atmosphere of the media center.

Answer: a. rewarded with grades or certificates for their service.

It is important to recognize students for the valuable service they perform as student library aides. In younger grades that recognition can come in the form or certificates. High school or middle school students may be a library aide as part of their course requirements. In this case, outstanding performance would be recognized in the form of grades. Option A is the most appropriate answer.

55.   **The most efficient method of evaluating support staff is to (Skill 3.5) Average Rigor**

a.   administer a written test.
b.   survey faculty whom they serve.
c.   observe their performance.
d.   obtain verbal confirmation during   an employee interview.

Answer: c. observe their performance

The most efficient method of evaluating support staff is to observe their performance. An observation can provide an overall picture of the tasks they routinely perform. Observations may be conducted by the media specialist alone or in conjunction with another school administrator or fellow media specialist.

56.   According to *Information Power*, which of the following is NOT a responsibility of the school library media specialist?
       (Skill 3.5) Rigorous

a.   maintaining and repairing equipment.
b.   instructing educators and parents in the use of library media resources.
c.   providing efficient retrieval systems for materials and equipment.
d.   planning and implementing the library media center budget.

Answer: a. maintaining and repairing equipment

While the school library media specialist is responsible for program administration and aiding with instruction, their responsibilities do not include maintaining and repairing equipment. This is generally the duty of an assistant or technician

57.   All of the following are areas in which the school library media specialist supports the learning community except
       (Skill 3.5) Average Rigor

a.   Technician
b.   Collaboration
c.   Leadership
d.   Technology

Answer: a. Technician

The school library media specialist should not have to serve in the capacity of a technician. They should work to collaborate with staff, provide leadership, and training on new technologies.

58.   A school with 500 – 749 students should have how many media specialists?
       (Skill 3.5) Easy

a.   1 part-time media specialist
b.   1 full time media specialist
c.   2 full time media specialist
d.   no media specialist required

Answer: b. 1 full time media specialist

It is recommended that schools with 500 to 749 students have at least 1 full time media specialist. This makes Option B the most appropriate response.

59. **Which of the following is the best description of the ALA recommendations for certification for a school library media specialist?**
(Skill 3.5) Easy

a. a bachelor's degree in any content area plus 30 hours of library/information science.
b. a master's degree from an accredited Educational Media program.
c. a bachelor's degree in library/ information science and a master's degree in any field of education.
d. a master's degree from an accredited Library and Information Studies program.

Answer: d. A master's degree from an accredited Library and Information Studies Program

According to the American Library Association to become a certified school librarian one should attain a master's degree from and ALA accredited Library and Information Studies Program. It is important to check a program's accreditation status before pursuing a degree at that institution. Some locations will not hire librarians who did not graduate from an accredited program.

60. **Which of these Dewey Decimal classifications should be weeded most often?**
(Skill 3.6) Rigorous

a. 100s
b. 500s
c. 700s
d. Biographies

Answer: b. 500s

Materials in this section need to be continuously checked to ensure that the scientific information is correct. The 100s should be weeded every five to eight years. The 700s should be kept until worn and biographies keep the most current versions.

61.   The process of discarding worn or outdated books and materials is known as:
        (Skill 3.6) Easy

a.   weeding
b.   inventory
c.   collection mapping
d.   eliminating

Answer: a. weeding

Option A is the most appropriate answer. Outdated or worn books and materials need to be removed from the library collection. This process is known as weeding

62.   An acronym that is often used to remind media specialists of the steps to weeding a collection is:
        (Skill 3.6) Average rigor

a.   WEAR
b.   MUSTIE
c.   ABCD
d.   RIPPED

Answer: b. MUSTIE

63.   A policy that provides guidelines for the use of the school or district's electronic resources and the consequences that occur if the resources are not used properly.
        (Skill 3.7) Easy

a.   Collection development policy
b.   Media selection policy
c.   Acceptable use policy
d.   None of the above

Answer: c. Acceptable use policy

An acceptable use policy outlines correct use of electronic resources. The most appropriate answer is Option C.

64. **Automated circulation systems have all of the following advantages except:**
   (Skill 3.8) Average rigor

a.   Require maintenance or original card catalog
b.   Provide quick access to circulation statistics
c.   Allow records to be searched easily
d.   Provide quick access to all collection resources

Answer: a. Require maintenance of original card catalog

Option A is the most appropriate answer. It is not necessary to maintain the original paper card catalog once the system is automated. Automated systems often provide a means to back-up the information electronically.

65. **A school library media specialist is searching for ways to make the school library more effective. Which of the following would not be a successful strategy?**
   (Skill 3.9) Rigorous

a.   The school library media specialist develops activities that help to develop creativity and support critical thinking skills.
b.   The school library media specialist works in isolation to plan effective programs that support curriculum guidelines.
c.   The school library media specialist develops activities to expand students' interests and promote lifelong learning.
d.   The school library media specialist provides physical access to resources.

Answer: b. The school library media specialist works in isolation to plan effective programs that support curriculum guidelines.

For a media program to be most effective, the media specialist should work closely with classroom teachers to form a strong collaborative partnership. While a media specialist may have to work in isolation to plan effective programs, it is not the most desired result. This makes Option B the most appropriate answer.

66.   A statement defining the core principles of a school library media program is called the:
       (Skill 3.9) Average rigor

a.   mission
b.   policy
c.   procedure
d.   objective

Answer: a. mission

The core principles of an organization are outlined in a mission statement. An objective is a specific statement of measurable result that reflects the mission statement.

67.   The role of the Media Committee or Media Advisory Committee is to assist with all of the following except:
       (Skill 3.9) Average rigor

a.   determine program direction
b.   evaluate the media specialist
c.   direct budget decisions
d.   collaborate with the media specialist

Answer: b. evaluate the media specialist

The Media Advisory Committee has the responsibility of helping to determine essential elements of the media collection, but they do not evaluate the media specialist.

68.   A general statement or outcome that is broken down into specific skills. This statement is known as a:
       (Skill 3.9) Average rigor

a.   policy
b.   procedure
c.   goal
d.   objective

Answer: c. goal

A goal is a general statement or outcome that is broken down into specific measurable objectives. Option C is the most appropriate answer.

69. **Long range plans should span how many years?**
    (Skill) Easy

a.   2 – 4
b.   3 – 5
c.   5 – 10
d.   10 – 15

Answer: b. 3-5

Long range plans should be developed to span from 3-5 years. It is important to record progress and plan periodic evaluations to determine which goals may need to be adjusted due to changing student populations and funding.

70. ***School Library Programs: Standards and Guidelines for Texas,*** **provides guidelines for exemplary media programs that include all of the following factors except:**
    (Skill 4.1) Average rigor

a.   Program evaluation occurs once per year.
b.   The program is student centered.
c.   A wide array of professional development is offered to meet individual needs.
d.   Parents are strongly encouraged to participate in learning activities.

Answer: a. Program evaluation occurs once per year.

Media program evaluation should be an ongoing process to ensure student needs are being met. The most appropriate answer is Option A.

71. A media specialist is working to ensure that the media program is meeting the exemplary requirements as outlined by *School Library Programs: Standards and Guidelines for Texas*. Which of the following best describes such a program?
     (Skill 4.1) Rigorous

a.   The media specialist has worked hard to find resources that meet curricular needs. There is adequate funding for building the collection. Even with her tightly fixed schedule the media specialist manages to meet with teachers occasionally. She has established a strong volunteer program to supplement the lack of adequate personnel.

b.   The media specialist has created a student-centered program that focuses on strong collaboration with the classroom teacher. She constantly evaluates the program to ensure the resources available support the program and meets the needs of the students.

c.   The media specialist collaborates with classroom teachers to ensure resources meet the needs of students. She has established partnerships within the community and a strong volunteer program to supplement the lack of adequate personnel.

d.   The media specialist has created a student-centered program that focuses on strong collaboration with the classroom teacher. Time for planning has been built into the fixed schedule allowing her to integrate information skills and technology into weekly lessons.

Answer: b. The media specialist has created a student-centered program that focuses on strong collaboration with the classroom teacher. She constantly evaluates the program to ensure the resources available support the program and meets the needs of the students.

The most appropriate answer is Option B. The other answers mention fixed instead of flexible schedules. For a media program to be considered exemplary it should have adequate staffing as well.

72.   Evaluation of a media program is crucial to its success. The data gathered during an evaluation can be beneficial for all of the following reasons except:
(Skill 4.2) Average rigor

a.   The data can be beneficial during the budgeting process to determine priorities.
b.   Identifies weakness and strengths of the resource collection.
c.   Can assist with informing the community of the needs of the program.
d.   Provides an outline for staff responsibilities.

Answer: d. Provides an outline for staff responsibilities

Option D is the most appropriate answer. Evaluation data can provide budget priorities, identify strengths and weaknesses and inform the community of program needs.

73.   As a good leader, the media specialist must exhibit certain qualities and perform certain duties. These include all of the following except:
(Skill 4.3) Easy

a.   Demonstrate appreciation for the work of others.
b.   Design and execute a media program on her own.
c.   Engage in continuing education.
d.   Maintain active memberships in professional organizations.

Answer: b. Design and execute a media program on her own

An effective leader learns to delegate responsibilities and works collaboratively with all staff to design and execute a media program. Option B is the most appropriate answer.

74. **The American Library Association strongly advocates the use of the school library media program to address and celebrate the diverse populations within a school. There are simple ways a media program can address this topic:**
    (Skill 4.4) Average rigor

a. Provide resources that address a variety of cultures. This should include both fiction and non-fiction works.
b. Plan celebrations that focus upon various cultures or student populations.
c. Invite guest speakers related to these topics.
d. All of the above

Answer: d. All of the above

Option D is the most appropriate answer. All of the answers listed are ways media specialists can address diversity within the media program.

75. **Effective communication is essential to a quality media program. Which of the following is a benefit of effective communication?**
    (Skill 4.5) Average rigor

a. Allows the media specialist to convey the mission and goals
b. Allows the media specialist to convey current research
c. Provides the media specialist with the skills to prepare effective reports.
d. All of the above

Answer: d. All of the above

Option D is the most appropriate answer. Effective communication is essential to the promotion of the media program.

76. **Partners for a school library media program may include:**
    (Skills 4.6) Easy

a.   universities
b.   local businesses
c.   community organizations
d.   all of the above

Answer: d. all of the above

Universities, local businesses, and community organizations are all viable partners for a media program. Universities may provide additional training for staff or open their resource catalog for use by local school districts. Local businesses often donate funds, equipment or professional expertise to local schools. Community organizations work to turn students into strong community leaders by providing programs and awards.

77. **Parent involvement is critical to the support of a school and media program. Which of the following is the least effective way to increase parent involvement:**
    (Skill 4.7)Easy

a.   Plan special family nights.
b.   Plan parent workshops
c.   Involve parents as volunteers.
d.   Send notes home to parents

Answer: d. Send notes home to parents

Sending notes home is not as effective as actually involving parents in school activities. Option D is the most appropriate answer.

78. **This outlines the role of the school library media specialist and the programs they manage.**
    (Skill 4.8) Average Rigor

a.   Taxonomies of Learning
b.   Code of Ethics
c.   @ Your Library
d.   Library Bill of Rights

Answer: c. @ Your Library

As part of ALA's Advocacy Toolkit, @ Your Library outlines the role of the school library media specialist and the programs they manage. This makes Option C the most appropriate response.

79. **Which version of *Information Power* was published in 1998?**
    (Skill 5.1) Easy

a. *Information Power: The Role of the School Library Media Program*
b. *Information Power: A Review of Research*
c. *Information Power: Guidelines for School Library Media Programs*
d. *Information Power: Building Partnerships for Learning*

Answer: d. *Information Power: Building Partnerships for Learning*

Option D is the version that was published in 1998. *Information Power: Guidelines for School Library Media Programs* was published in 1988.

80. **All of the following organizations serve school libraries except:**
    (Skill 5.1) Average Rigor

a. AASL
b. AECT
c. ALCT
d. ALA

Answer: c. ALCT

The American Association of School Librarians (AASL), The Association for Educational Communications and Technology (AECT), and the American Library Association (ALA) are all organizations that support and serve school libraries.

81. **National guidelines for school library media programs are generally developed by all of the following except:**
    (Skill 5.1) Easy

a. AASL
b. ALA
c. AECT
d. NECT

Answer: d. NECT

AASL, ALA, and AECT assist with developing guidelines for school library media centers. Option D is the most appropriate answer.

82.   School libraries have moved away from simply housing a collection of resources to serving as the central element of the school. The school library media program serves to provide students with the information they need to become lifelong learning.

All are key factors that influence this role except:
(Skill 5.2) Rigorous

a.   The development of a program that supports authentic learning experiences.
b.   The program must include accommodations for volunteers.
c.   Full administrative support.
d.   Effective integration of information literacy skills into the curriculum.

Answer: b. The program must include accommodations for volunteers

Accommodating volunteers is not a factor that influences the role of the media specialist. The most appropriate answer is Option B

83.   Which of the following is NOT one of three general criteria for selection of all materials?
(Skill 5.3) Average Rigor

a.   authenticity.
b.   appeal.
c.   appropriateness.
d.   allocation.

Answer: d. allocation

When selecting materials the school library generally looks for materials that have reliable information, appeal to students and are appropriate for the grade levels their program serves. Option D, allocation, is not one of the criteria use to select materials

84. **Collection development policies are developed to accomplish all of the following except**
   (Skill 5.3) Rigorous

a. guarantee users freedom to access information.
b. recognize the needs and interests of users.
c. coordinate selection criteria and budget concerns.
d. recognize rights of individuals or groups to challenge these policies.

Answer: c. coordinate selection criteria and budget concerns

The main goal of a collection development policy is to set guidelines and procedures that govern how resources are purchased and managed. It does not coordinate any criteria or address funding issues.

85. **When selecting books for students in grades k-2, it is best to choose books with which of the following characteristics?**
   (Skill 5.3) Easy

a. strong picture support
b. familiar language patterns
c. utilize cuing systems
d. all of the above

Answer: d. all of the above

The best answer is Option D. Young readers need books that have strong picture support, repetitive language patterns, and strong cuing systems.

86. **MARC is the acronym for:**
   (Skill 5.4) Easy

a. Mobile Accessible Recorded Content
b. Machine Accessible Readable Content
c. Machine Readable Content
d. Mobile Accessible Readable Content

Answer: c. Machine Readable Content

Option C is the most appropriate answer. MARC is the acronym for Machine Readable Content. The MARC format is used in the cataloging of resources.

87.   **In MARC records the title information can be found under which tag?**
        (Skill 5.5) Rigorous

a.   130
b.   245
c.   425
d.   520

Answer: b. 245

The 245 tag is where the title information is recorded in a MARC record. Option B is the most appropriate response. The 520 tag is where the summary is listed.

88.   **In which bibliographic field should information concerning the**
        format of an audio-visual material appear?
        (Skill 5.5) Rigorous

a.   Material specific details.
b.   Physical description.
c.   Notes.
d.   Standard numbers.

Answer: c. Notes

Using the 500 – General Note field in a MARC record the format of the audio-visual materials can be listed. This makes Option C the most appropriate answer. The physical description contains information about the price and number of pages.

89.   **AACR2 is the acronym for:**
        (Skill 5.5) Easy

a.   Anglo-American Cataloging Rules Second Edition
b.   American Association of Cataloging Rules Second Edition
c.   American Association of Content Rules Second Edition
d.   Anglo-American Content Rules Second Edition

Answer: a. Anglo-American Cataloging Rules Second Edition

Option A is the most appropriate answer. AACR2 outlines specific rules that must be followed when cataloging items.

90. **OCLC is the acronym for:**
(Skill 5.5) Average Rigor

a. Online Computer Library Center
b. Online Computer Library Catalog
c. Online Computer Library Conference
d. Online Computer Library Content

Answer: a. Online Computer Library Center

The most appropriate answer is Option A, the Online Computer Library Center. This center provides bibliographic (MARC) records.

91. **Which of the following is not a component of a bibliographic record?**
(Skill 5.5) Rigorous

a. Notes
b. Call number
c. Cover image
d. Physical description area

Answer: c. cover image

The cover image would be a detail listed under one of the components in a bibliographic record. It is not a component itself, making Option C the most appropriate response.

92. **A periodical index search which allows the user to pair Keywords with and, but, or or is called**
(Skill 5.6) Average Rigor

a. Boolean.
b. dialoguing.
c. wildcarding.
d. truncation.

Answer: a. Boolean

The most appropriate answer is Option A, Boolean. A Boolean search uses keywords along with terms such as and, but, and or, to define the search. Wildcarding is a form of searching that uses something such as an asterisks to find different formats of words or terms.

93. **Which of the following searches would most likely return the most results?**
(Skill 5.6) Average Rigor

a. lions and tigers
b. lions not tigers
c. lions or tigers
d. lions and not tigers

Answer: c. Lions or tigers.

The use of OR in the search lets the search engine know to find articles that contain either of the words listed. With the use of AND, the search engine will look for articles that have both words in the article.

94. **A search that uses specific terms to locate information is called a:**
(Skill 5.6) Average rigor

a. reference search
b. keyword search
c. ready reference search
d. operator search

Answer: b. keyword search

A keyword search uses specific terms to locate information. The most appropriate answer is Option B.

95. **A request from a social studies for the creation of a list of historical fiction titles for a book report assignment is a _____ request.**
(Skill 5.7) Rigorous

a. ready reference.
b. research.
c. specific needs.
d. complex search.

Answer: c. specific needs.

Requests made for particular titles or resources are known as a special needs request. Option C is the most appropriate answer.

96.   When working with patrons to determine their specific information needs it may be necessary to ask the patron a series of questions that uncover needs, often called a:
        (Skill 5.7) Rigorous

a.   ready reference request
b.   special needs request
c.   reference interview
d   evaluation interview

Answer: c. reference interview

A reference interview may be necessary to determine the specific needs of the patron. A reference interview consists of asking the patron a series of open-ended questions that assist in narrowing the topic. This makes Option C the most appropriate answer.

97.   Which of the following would be a good question to ask during a reference interview?
        (Skill 5.7) Rigorous

a.   Do you have a topic?
b.   What is your topic?
c.   Have you located any resources regarding your topic?
d.   Do you know where to go to find the information?

Answer: b. What is your topic?

The most appropriate reference interview questions are open-ended making Option B the most appropriate answer. It is the only question that requires more than a yes or no answer.

98.   All of the following are periodical directories except:
        (Skill 5.8) Average Rigor

a.   *Ulrich's*
b.   *TNYT*
c.   *SIRS*
d.   *PAIS*

Answer: b. TNYT

Option B is the most appropriate answer. All of the other are directories listed are specifically for periodicals.

99. **Which professional journal is published by the American Association of School Librarians?**
(Skill 5.8) Average Rigor

a. *School Library Media Research*
b. *Library Trends*
c. *Library Power*
d. *Voices of Youth Advocate*

Answer: a. *School Library Media Research*

The only journal listed that is published by the AASL is *School Library Media Research*. This makes Option A the most appropriate response.

100. **The program that is used to encourage students to read during the summer months is called:**
(Skill 5.9) Easy

a. Texas Reading Club
b. Bluebonnet Reading Club
c. Lone Star Reading Club
d. None of the above

Answer: a. Texas Reading Club

Special programs such as the Texas Reading Club encourage students to read during the summer months. Students who complete the program are recognized.

101. **A student looks for a specific title on domestic violence. When he learns it is overdue, he asks the library media specialist to tell him the borrower's name. The library media specialist should first**
(Skill 5.10) Rigorous

a. readily reveal the borrower's name.
b. suggest he look for the book in another library.
c. offer to put the boy's name on reserve pending the book's return.
d. offer to request an interlibrary loan.

Answer: c. Offer to put the boy's name on reserve pending the book's return.

Patron confidentiality is of the utmost importance. The media specialist also needs to meet the needs of the patron requesting the book. The most appropriate course of action is Option C, offer to put the boy's name on reserve pending the book's return.

102. **The Right to Read Statement was issued by:**
(Skill 5.10) Rigorous

a.   AECT
b.   ALA
c.   NCTE
d.   NICEM

Answer: c. NCTE.

The National Council of Teachers of English (NCTE) is responsible for the creation of the Right to Read Statement. This make Option C the most appropriate answer.

103. **All of the following are state library and technology organizations except:**
(Skill 5.11) Average rigor

a.   TCEA
b.   TAET
c.   TLA
d.   TASL

Answer: b. TAET

The following are state level media and technology organizations:
    Texas Computer Education Association (TCEA)
    Texas Library Association (TLA)
    Texas Association of School Librarians (TASL)

104. **Which of the following is not a national organization that supports media and technology efforts:**
(Skill 5.11) Rigorous

a.   NCTM
b.   ALA
c.   AASL
d.   ASCD

Answer: a. NCTM

The following are national organizations that support media and technology efforts.
    American Library Association (ALA)
    American Association of School Library (AASL)
    Association for Supervision and Curriculum Development (ASCD)

105. **Which of the following file extensions does not represent an image file?**
(Skill 6.1) Average Rigor

a. .jpeg
b. .gif
c. .csv
d. .bmp

Answer: c. .csv

Image file types can be .jpeg or .jpg, .gif, .png, and .bmp to name a few. The .csv file stands for comma separated value and is usually associated with a spreadsheet. Other file types are .doc for word processed documents, .txt for text files, .mdb or .db are database files.

106. **A group of students in the business club will be creating a website to sell their product. When selecting their domain name, which of the following extensions would be best to use?**
(Skill 6.1) Rigorous

a. .com
b. .edu
c. .cfm
d. .html

Answer: a. .com

A website that is used for commercial purposes should have a .com extension. The domain name is the location where the web page information is stored. Because the question specifically stated the domain name, Option A is the most appropriate answer. The .edu extension is used for educational institutions. The .html extension refers to the programming used to create a web page and stands for hypertext mark-up language.

107. **Which of the following is not a criterion used to evaluate resources for a media collection?**
(Skill 6.2) Easy

a. Audience
b. Scope
c. Accuracy
d. All of the above

Answer: d. All of the above

All of the options should be considered when evaluating resources for a media collection. Option D is the most appropriate answer.

108. **Instruction provided via satellite or cable television is called**
(Skill 6.3) Average Rigor

a. home study.
b. distance learning.
c. extension services.
d. telecommunications.

Answer: b. distance learning

To make the most of funding dollars many school districts have turned to courses offered via satellite, cable or online. Through these initiatives students can have access to a wider array of courses that many small districts may not be able to fund. The most appropriate answer is Option B, distance learning.

109. **Advantages of distance education include all of the following except:**
(Skill 6.3) Rigorous

a. students can access and respond to information outside of a normal schedule.
b. students have fewer choices regarding content.
c. homebound students may receive instruction.
d. it may be more cost effective to use distance learning than to hire a teacher

Answer: b. students have fewer choices regarding content

The use of distance learning classes actually expands the opportunities students have regarding content. The most appropriate answer is Option B.

110. **When allowing interlibrary loan with a public library, which item should be taken into consideration?**
      (Skill 6.4) Rigorous

a.   Where the item will be housed?
b.   How will funds be distributed?
c.   How personnel will be distributed.
d.   None of the above

Answer: d. None of the above

When establishing interlibrary loan with a public library the main consideration is how to make collections available to patrons. Each entity generally maintains their collection, funding and personnel. Option D is the most appropriate answer.

111. **Web page editing software that allows the user to preview web pages as they are being created is called:**
      (Skill 6.5) Average rigor

a.   WYSWYG
b.   WYSIYG
c.   WISWYG
d.   WYSIWYG

Answer: d. WYSIWYG

The correct answer is Option D. Web page editing software that allows users to preview web pages as they are being created is called WYSIWYG software or What You See Is What You Get.

112. **Software designed to organize, manage and retrieve resources quickly and easily is called:**
      (Skill 6.5) Average rigor

a.   database
b.   spreadsheet
c.   word processing
d.   teleconference

Answer: a database

Databases are used to organize, manage and retrieve resources quickly, making Option A the most appropriate answer. While spreadsheets are able to perform those tasks, their primary purpose is to perform calculations.

113. **Software that allows users to communicate over the Internet using audio and/or video is called:**
(Skill 6.5) Rigorous

a. database
b. spreadsheet
c. web editor
d. teleconferencing

Answer: d. teleconferencing

Teleconferencing software and equipment allows video and/ or audio to be broadcast online for the purpose of communicating with others. Option D is the most appropriate answer.

114. **Texas Essential Knowledge and Skills (TEKS) stress the importance of integrating information and technology skills to assist with problem-solving processes. There are three main areas where technology works with this process. Which is not an example?**
(Skill 6.6) Rigorous

a. Use appropriate technology to modify the solution to problems.
b. Use technology to communicate with others and enhance research skills.
c. Use technology to locate and use information.
d. Use technology to evaluate both the process and product of information learned.

Answer: c. Use technology to locate and use information

Option C is the most appropriate answer. All other options are examples of how technology assists with the problem solving process.

115. The media specialist is searching a database and needs to locate all of the entries that begin with the letter "P". What is the best way to format this search?
(Skill 6.7) Rigorous

a.   Create a search using the Boolean operator AND NOT. (P AND NOT A, B, C, D, E...)
b.   Place quotations around the letter P
c.   Use a wildcard
d.   This type of search cannot be done.

Answer: c. Use a wildcard

This is an effective tool if one is unsure of the spelling or date for the topic being searched. . One way to phrase the search is to type P* . The asterisk at the end will cause the search to return anything in the database that begins with the letters "P".

116. In the production of a teacher/student made audio-visual material, which of the following is NOT a factor in the planning phase?
(Skill 6.8) Rigorous

a.   stating the objectives.
b.   analyzing the audience.
c.   determining the purpose.
d.   selecting the format.

Answer: d. selecting the format.
During the planning phase it is necessary to determine who the information is designed for. The determining of the format comes later.

117. Which of the following formats is best for large group presentations?
(Skill 6.8) Easy

a.   manipulatives
b.   multimedia
c.   audio recordings
d.   photographs

Answer: b. multimedia

Multimedia presentations are most appropriate for large groups. When used in conjunction with projectors and large screens, multimedia presentations are very effective.

118. All of the following formats are best for small group learning except:
      (Skill 6.8) Average rigor

a.   manipulatives
b.   computer projection
c.   photographs
d.   computer software

Answer: d. computer software

Computer software used on a single machine is most appropriate for small groups. The most appropriate answer is Option D.

119. The school library media specialist is responsible for helping to prepare students to be 21st century citizen. An important part of this process is to stay abreast of the technology initiatives at various levels. All of the following can assist with this process except:
      (Skill 6.9) Average rigor

a.   subscribing to newsletters
b.   sending newsletters to staff
c.   participating in library related discussion boards
d.   actively participating in state and national library associations

Answer: b. sending newsletters to staff

This is a way to keep staff current, but is not a means for the media specialist to gain information. Option B is the most appropriate answer.

120. The acronym OPAC stands for:
      (Skill 6.10) Average rigor

a.   Online Public Access Catalogs
b.   Organization for Public Accessible Catalogs
c.   Online Patron Accessible Catalogs
d.   Organization for Public Access Catalogs

Answer: a. Online Public Access Catalogs

Online Public Access Catalogs allow patrons to find information via the web. This allows for anytime anywhere access of resources. Option A is the most appropriate answer.

121. **In a school with one full-time library media assistant (clerk), which of the following are responsibilities of the assistant?**
(Skill 3.5) *Average rigor*

a. selecting and ordering titles for the print collection.
b. performing circulation tasks and processing new materials.
c. inservicing teachers on the integration of media materials into the school curriculum.
d. planning and implementing programs to involve parents and community

Answer: b. performing circulation tasks and processing new materials.

Option B is the most appropriate answer. Circulation tasks and the processing of materials generally involve clerical duties. The other options are usually performed by a licensed media specialists.

122. **Which periodical contains book reviews of currently published children and young adult books?**
(Skill 5.8) *Rigorous*

a. *Phi Delta Kappan*
b. *School Library Journal*
c. *School Library Media Quarterly*
d. *American Teacher*

Answer: b. School Library Journal

The *School Library Journal* is the world's largest book review source making Option B the best answer. *Phi Delta Kappan* is a professional journal for education. *School Library Media Quarterly* is a journal published by the American Library Association to assist with program administration of school library media programs. *American Teacher* is a magazine for the teaching profession.

123. **It is often necessary that equipment be shared amongst teachers. The equipment can be checked out from the media center. Which of the following is necessary for the use and transporting of equipment?**
     (Skill 3.4) Rigorous

a. Directions for use
b. Straps or lock-downs to secure items being transported
c. Having a staff member on hand to assist with set up.
d. None of the above.

Answer: b. Straps or lock-downs to secure items being transported

It is crucial that portable equipment is secure when being transported to avoid injury. The other items are good to provide, but not necessary. Option B is the most appropriate answer.

124. **Collaborative partnerships with staff can take on many forms. All of the following are examples except:**
     (Skill 3.9) Rigorous

a. serving on curriculum development committees
b. viewing the school's curriculum and creating lessons
c. assisting teachers in planning, designing, and teaching lessons
d. assisting teachers and students with the use of new technologies

Answer: b. viewing the school's curriculum and creating lessons

For the collaborative process to be effective the media specialist needs to work closely with the classroom teacher to create and plan lessons. The planning should not be conducted by the media specialist alone. This may occur, but it is not the desired result. Option B is the most appropriate answer.

125. **When implementing new technologies it is important for the media specialist to model its use. It is also important for the media specialist to:**
(Skill 6.7) Average rigor

a.   Send updated hand-outs to staff.
b.   Provide web resources to assist with utilization of the tool.
c.   Provide brief refresher modules.
d.   All of the above.

Answer: d. all of the above

Staff are more responsive and tend to utilize new technologies more when they know they have support when they need it most. Option D is the most appropriate answer because all three play an important role in that process.

XAMonline, INC. 21 Orient Ave. Melrose, MA 02176

Toll Free number 800-509-4128

TO ORDER Fax 781-662-9268 OR www.XAMonline.com

TEXAS EXAMINATION OF EDUCATOR STANDARDS- EXAMINATION FOR THE CERTIFICATION OF EDUCATORS - TEXES/EXCET - 2007

PO#   Store/School:

Address 1:

Address 2 (Ship to other):

City, State Zip

Credit card number_____-_____-_____-_____   expiration_____

EMAIL _____

PHONE   **FAX**

13# ISBN 2007	TITLE	Qty	Retail	Total
978-1-58197-925-1	ExCET ART SAMPLE TEST (ALL-LEVEL-SECONDARY) 005 006			
978-1-58197-949-7	TExES CHEMISTRY 8-12 140			
978-1-58197-938-1	TExES COMPUTER SCIENCE 141			
978-1-58197-933-6	TExES ENGLISH LANG-ARTS AND READING 4-8 117			
978-1-58197-935-0	TExES ENGLISH LANG-ARTS AND READING 8-12 131			
978-1-58197-926-8	ExCET FRENCH SAMPLE TEST (SECONDARY) 048			
978-1-58197-605-2	TExES GENERALIST 4-8 111			
978-1-58197-945-9	TExES GENERALIST EC-4 101			
978-1-58197-946-6	TExES SCIENCE 4-8 116			
978-1-58197-931-2	TExES SCIENCE 8-12 136			
978-1-58197-604-5	TExES LIFE SCIENCE 8-12 138			
978-1-58197-932-9	TExES MATHEMATICS 4-8 114-115			
978-1-58197-937-4	TExES MATHEMATICS 8-12 135			
978-1-58197-939-8	TExES MATHEMATICS-PHYSICS 8-12 143			
978-1-58197-948-0	TExES MATHEMATICS-SCIENCE 4-8 114			
978-1-58197-929-9	TExES PEDAGOGY AND PROFESSIONAL RESPONSIBILITIES 4-8 110			
978-1-58197-899-5	TExES PEDAGOGY AND PROFESSIONAL RESPONSIBILITIES EC-4 100			
978-1-58197-943-5	TExES PHYSICAL EDUCATON EC-12 158			
978-1-58197-928-2	TExES PRINCIPAL 068			
978-1-58197-941-1	TExES READING SPECIALIST 151			
978-1-58197-942-8	TExES SCHOOL COUNSELOR 152			
978-1-58197-940-4	TExES SCHOOL LIBRARIAN 150			
978-1-58197-934-3	TExES SOCIAL STUDIES 4-8 118			
978-1-58197-936-7	TExES SOCIAL STUDIES 8-12 132			
978-1-58197-927-5	ExCET SPANISH (SECONDARY) 047			
978-1-58197-944-2	TExES SPECIAL EDUCATION EC-12 161			
978-1-58197-606-9	THEA TEXAS HIGHER EDUCATOR ASSESSMENT			

FOR PRODUCT PRICES GO TO WWW.XAMONLINE.COM	**SUBTOTAL**
	Ship $8.25
	TOTAL

CPSIA information can be obtained at www.ICGtesting.com
Printed in the USA
LVOW09s1050070615

441504LV00011B/612/P

9 781581 979404